BRAINSTORMING YOUR NOVEL

FROM FIRST SPARK TO BLOCKBUSTER

LINDA NEEDHAM

BIG SCRUMPY PRESS

Every bestselling story begins with an idea.
But in the highly competitive publishing market how does a writer
decide which ideas need telling and which stories to tell?

As every writer knows, an idea is not a story. It's merely a spark, a memory, a current or historical event, a snapshot, an insight, a family story, a feeling.

Ideas! We writers see them everywhere. But sorting through the clutter of ideas for the one that suggests the greatest story potential can be painful, time-consuming and frustrating.

From First Spark to Blockbuster takes the pain out of brainstorming your next book! You'll learn how to:

- Brainstorm the Origins of your Idea
- Reveal Why your Idea has Meaning to you
- Compile a List of Theme Words
- Develop a Dynamic Premise
- Orchestrate a Robust Cast of Characters
- Devise an Elevator Pitch

Join award-winning, *USA Today* Bestselling author, Linda Needham in this interactive brainstorming workshop-in-a-book, and turn your First Spark of an Idea into a Blockbuster work of fiction

Brainstorming Your Novel:
From First Spark to Blockbuster

THE ORIGIN

I first shared the early version of my brainstorming process way back in 1997 at a meeting of my local chapter of Romance Writers of America. As a follow-up, I wrote a condensed version for a two-part article in the chapter's newsletter. By 1999, I had developed my process into a full workshop and presented it at the RWA Conference in Chicago.

The original conference program blurb read:

> *Whether plot or setting or character comes to you first, here's an in-depth, hands-on session that will help you explore your Story Idea for compelling, character-based conflict.*

My brainstorming workshop proved to be so popular that I presented it a few dozen times over the following years, sharing the process with many other writers, in-person, and in a variety of settings, including libraries, bookstores, writer's groups, and conferences.

The workshop was intensely hands-on and in-depth, minus the stress of composing on the spot because, being a plotter, I suck at writing prompts. Though sharing among the attendees was integral to the workshop, I made sure that no one ever felt pressured to share or reveal their work.

We would start the process with everyone jotting down–no composing, please–a story idea that has been pestering them to be told. A few brave volunteers would share the spark of their Idea, focusing on just the spark, not the meaning.

Brainstorming the Meaning came next. I gave the attendees a few minutes to jot down (again *just jotting*) a list of all the reasons they were so intrigued by this spark. The initial volunteers would then remind us of their Ideas, then shared the jotted Meaning that spoke loudest to them.

Invariably, at least three additional writers would volunteer their Ideas and their Meanings. Each shared Idea would spark another, building enthusiasm for the brainstorming process.

Confirming the definition of Brainstorming from *Merriam-Webster*:

> *The mulling over of ideas by one or more individuals in an attempt to devise or find a solution to a problem.*

More brainstorming would follow as we eagerly shared Theme Words, Premises, Characters, and Elevator Pitches, each new spark igniting new journeys, and illuminating new vistas.

At the end of every workshop session, the writers would stagger away, faces flushed with inspiration, eyes bright with the light of story, that tiny spark of an idea now fanned into a raging inferno. And I loved every minute of it! Loved sharing my brainstorming process with other writers in those live interactive sessions.

THE SPARK

A fabulous and fun workshop, packed with writerly inspiration that I wanted to share with every writer, everywhere. But for years

I had no possible way to deliver it, except in-person. How could I recreate a highly interactive, hands-on brainstorming workshop without you and me being in the same conference room? I'm happy to say that, now, thanks to all things digital, I've found a way!

First Spark is my original brainstorming workshop, in book form. A step-by-step guide through the process that I use, not only for my in-person sessions, but also to develop my own stories.

And we won't be alone on our journey! We'll be joined at every step by the four Volunteer Brainstorming Avatars I created to replicate the workshop experience, which will give you a more in-depth look at each step in the process. Two examples are based on actual workshop attendees, one on a friend, and one is my own. I also share examples from a few of my own bestsellers in each of the six steps. So there'll be plenty of sharing going on.

Thanks so much for purchasing *From First Spark to Blockbuster.* Let's set your story Idea on fire!

A Huge Thank You

~ To my dear husband of 33 years, my partner in publishing, the love of my life, the laughter in my heart—you are the best part of me.

~ To my family—James, Brit, Lorelai, and Kai, I love you to the moon and back.

~ To Sue and Pete, your adventures inspire me!

~ To Alexa Haddock Bigwarfe and the Women in Publishing community for your invaluable encouragement; and to the Tiny Book panel at the 2022 Virtual Summit for convincing me to publish my old brainstorming workshop as a book to share with the writing world.

~ And to all the writers over the past 25 years who attended my Great Ideas workshops. You taught me more than you can imagine. Without your help in its Origins, First Spark would still be just an unexplored Idea.

BRAINSTORMING YOUR NOVEL

CONTENTS

WHERE DO YOU GET YOUR IDEAS?

THE QUESTION

"Oh, you're a writer!" exclaims a starry-eyed parent at your daughter's basketball game. "Where do you get your ideas?"

Ouch! I mean, how are you supposed to answer on the spot when a non-writerly type ambushes you with that question?

Especially when asked, with a knowing smirk, by your ex-boyfriend at your 20th high school reunion.

Or by the plumber who's come to repair your washing machine, who declares he doesn't read books.

Or at your cousin's wedding.

Even worse, the question is asked by your favorite aunt's creepy new boyfriend, who has a great idea for a story about a dead body that he and his buddies found in a ditch when he was 13. (Uhmm, you think, *Stand By Me*?)

To add to your discomfort, he generously assures you that if *you* write the story, he'll split the profits, 50-50. What a deal!

Been there, right?

Still, no matter who asks you the question, it's difficult to answer. Even after my 25 years in the writing business, with a dozen published novels, both traditional and indie, with five books appearing on the USA Today Bestseller list, and many awards, you'd think the answer to that imponderable question—*where do you get your ideas?*—would roll off my tongue as easily as my own name.

It doesn't. I'm always stumped for a clear and simple answer that doesn't come out sounding super snarky, like:

- Ideas? I get 'em for $7.99 a pound in the bulk aisle at Whole Foods.
- From my fairy god-editor
- From the Writer's Digest Idea-of-the-Month Club

See, definitely snarky.

But I really don't know how to answer the *where* question, because, as we writerly types all know, an *idea* is not a story. *Where* an idea comes from doesn't matter at all; what the heck we *do* with the idea means everything!

Wherever the idea comes from, it's merely a spark, a snippet, a memory, a current or historic event, a snapshot, an insight, a family story, a feeling.

It's an iceberg that sinks an unsinkable passenger ship on a crystal clear night in the North Atlantic.

But an iceberg that sinks an unsinkable ship isn't a story. It's still just an idea. A what-if.

An historical event that lacks the ill-fated, forbidden romance between the beautiful, young, upper-class Rose DeWitt and the free-spirited steerage passenger Jack Dawson who, in that short voyage, teaches Rose that "life is a gift", that she must "make every day count" and, with his heroic dying breath makes her promise she will survive the icy waters and never give up on her life, no matter how dark or hopeless things become, giving Rose the courage to throw off the shackles of the suffocating Edwardian society that held her prisoner and, in the decades that followed, to make her life count.

James Cameron's *Titanic* is a fully realized story that came from a simple historical event. An idea.

The truth is that ideas are ubiquitous. We writers see them everywhere, even when we're not looking for them.
Here's the definition of Idea from Dictionary.com.

noun. any conception existing in the mind as a result of mental under-standing, awareness, or activity. a thought, conception, or notion.

For a fiction writer, an idea is just the spark that sets off a dynamic process in the creation of a story, one that must eventually include engaging characters and their riveting story arcs, unimaginable stakes and thrilling plot lines, images and themes, bursting with evocative settings, dramatic dialog, and all the other elements that make up a blockbuster story.

Once you've settled on one of the millions of ideas shouting at you from your file folder—or wherever you lock away such items—how can you tell if that idea will be robust enough to withstand the rigors of carrying an entire story? How do you move your Idea from Spark to What-if to the Bestseller List, let alone to finishing your manuscript and typing "The End?"

Since every part of a story exists solely in service to the protagonist and their journey, we need to choose our Ideas and What-ifs wisely. The choice I make is a promise to my readers that my characters will storm ruthlessly through the pages of their story, in a life-and-death battle between innocence and evil, right and righter, wrong or even wronger.

Here are loglines from three of my books:

- A young woman risks everything to lead an insurrection against those who seek to abolish the free press and silence free speech. (*My Wicked Earl*)

- A mission-hardened intelligence officer is forced to play nanny to an exiled princess. (*A Scandal to Remember*)
- A farmer on the English home front goes to battle to protect her family's estate from the Blitz, wartime shortages, and an invasion by the Royal Engineers. (*The Legend of Nimway Hall: 1940-Josie*)

My readers deserve nothing less than a fiercely motivated, conflicted protagonist who can't reach her final goal until she confronts her misbeliefs, overcomes her innermost fears, and becomes a new kind of person who could not have reached that goal without having first set out upon, and survived, the emotionally dangerous journey.

All of which we must magically create from that tiny spark, the unformed germ of an idea.

ABOUT THE BRAINSTORMING PROCESS

Because I work best taking simple, understandable steps toward my goal, I've organized the brainstorming process into six steps:

1. Jotting your Idea
2. Brainstorming the Meaning of your Idea
3. Brainstorming Theme Words
4. Brainstorming the Premise
5. Brainstorming Character Types
6. Brainstorming the Elevator Pitch

For our purposes, brainstorming is an exercise in positive, creative freedom, where nothing is wrong and everything is right. Where every new idea becomes a deposit in your bank of possibilities.

Come join me in an interactive brainstorming workshop and learn how to turn your first spark of an Idea from a What-if into a best-selling work of fiction.

STEP 1
the First Spark of Your Idea

How many times have you started writing a story because you overheard some tantalizing tidbit while eating dinner at a Red Robin? Perhaps it's an argument between a man and a woman in the next booth?

But your writerly imagination can't help casting these two ordinary diners as undercover CIA agents bickering over their current case…

Yeah, oh, and these two used to be married to each other, but, uhm, they divorced because his interfering mother moved in with them and kept rearranging the furniture, and now they are on a stakeout together…

… in Stockholm …
… posing as a maid and butler in the …
… the … Russian Embassy ….

Bam! The idea grabs you and doesn't let go!

So you rush home and start pounding away on your keyboard, burning gallons of midnight oil on a story about sexy spies, double-crosses, a stolen Rembrandt, decorating hints, a video that goes viral….

You write scene after scene after fevered scene until … until you realize your characters have ground to a stop ... and now refuse to go on. Not only are they boring, they're bored with each other, and worst of all, they're bored with you!

Because you didn't realize when you started writing this Red Robin comedy/thriller that all you really had was an idea, not a story. So you stop writing.

Sigh. Been there. Wrote that. What a waste of precious writing time, energy, and emotional investment. Stopping so abruptly may even have discouraged you from the idea itself, or worse, from ever writing again. That would be sad. And so unnecessary.

Okay, so what do we do when our attention is grabbed by an idea that begs to be explored?

- By a fascinating human interest news story about a 24-hour lending library located on the edge of an Oregon forest.
- Or a young boy growing up in a multi-generational family of pyrotechnicians.
- Or your great-grandfather's World War I diary written after the Battle of the Somme ....

These are just three ideas out of a zillion that have intrigued me over the years. Sparks. Story seeds. Touchstones.

To begin the brainstorming process, reach into your jam-packed bag of ideas and choose the one that you find the most engaging, the brightest spark that keeps igniting your imagination.

Your Idea in hand, the next step is to begin to understand the reason you chose that particular idea—the Origin of your interest. It's critically important to know this, because the deeper your emotional connection to the spark of your idea, the more powerful your story will be for your readers.

Ideas like those below can evoke a natural emotional reaction in writers and their readers alike:

- The struggles/adventures of yourself or a family member
- A personal hero, a public hero
- An outrage, an unresolved wrong
- An unthinkable loss
- A personal triumph
- A historical event with current resonance
- A personal memoir

Here's an example of the Origin and Idea of my historical romance *Once Upon a Treasure Hunt* (original title: *The Wedding Night*).

Example from:
ONCE UPON *a*
TREASURE HUNT

THE ORIGIN

The idea first engaged me while I was reading the introduction to *The Fairy Faith in Celtic Countries*, a 1910 book of field evidence gathered by W. Y. Evans-Wentz. The author was bemoaning the fact that folklore scholars, as well as their offbeat social science, were shunned by 'serious' academics at the time.

THE IDEA

A Victorian folklorist struggles to have her research taken seriously among cynical academics.

With my example in mind, it's time to meet our four brave Volunteer Brainstormers, who have eagerly shared their examples of Origins and Ideas in the following section.

Reminder: If we were together in my writer's workshop, at this point in my presentation, I would ask a few attendees to read their Origins and their Ideas aloud.

Since we are not together, I hope examples from our four Volunteer Brainstormers will serve as the next best thing.

THE ORIGINS AND IDEAS EXERCISE
FROM OUR VOLUNTEER BRAINSTORMERS

THE EXERCISE:

Briefly—very briefly—describe a setting, situation, character, or event that has intrigued you enough to consider creating a story around it.

Just jot. Don't compose—jot, jot, jot!
This isn't a writing exercise, the raw Idea only.

Example 1
The Vanishing Cyclist

THE ORIGIN:

A writer who attended one of my workshops shared the spark of an idea that had followed her for years: From her position at a rest stop off the highway, the writer saw a bicyclist enter a short car tunnel carved into a California hillside. As cars occasionally entered and exited, she watched and waited for the cyclist to appear at the opposite end, but he never did.

THE IDEA:

A bicyclist enters a car tunnel and vanishes.

Example 2
Library in the Woods

THE ORIGIN:

Decades ago I became enchanted by a local TV news story about a retired librarian who opened a free, 24/7 lending library in a charming, vintage Airstream trailer on her woodland property, which served her rural neighbors who couldn't get into town during regular library hours.

THE IDEA:

A 24-hour lending library in the woods.

Example 3
One Heiress Too Many

THE ORIGIN:

As I learned while watching the *Showtime* series *The Tudors*, Henry VIII's fifth wife, the doomed Catherine Howard (beheaded), had grown up as a ward of her father's stepmother, the Dowager Duchess of Norfolk. Supervision was lax in the household, which included a dozen other children of various nobles, each sent to the Dowager to be educated and trained up in the ways of the nobility.

THE IDEA:

Warehousing the inconvenient sons and daughters of the nobility in a chaotic household far from home.

Example 4
Diary of a Honeymoon

THE ORIGIN:

A number of years ago a close friend was given her great-aunt's letters, written in 1926 during her 2-month long, cross-county honeymoon/ husband's hospitality-industry business trip.

The extended honeymoon was a working trip, financed by the hospitality company the groom worked for at the time. His assignment was to leave holiday brochures in every motel along the ever-expanding network of paved roadways, made newly accessible to a growing number of ordinary folks by Henry Ford's affordable motor cars.

The bride mailed most of her letters to family members, asking them to save them for her. She also collected ephemera along the route—matchbooks, soap wrappers, postcards, local guides, maps, etc.

THE IDEA:

The travel diary adventures of a young couple embarking on their marriage.

Now it's your turn to choose your best Idea!

THE SPARK OF YOUR IDEA EXERCISE
~ BRAINSTORMING WORKSHEET~

Briefly—very briefly—describe a setting, situation, character, event, or anything at all that has intrigued you enough to consider creating a story around it.

Just jot! Don't compose—jot, jot, jot! This isn't a writing exercise. The basic Idea only.

THE ORIGIN:

YOUR IDEA:

STEP 2
The Meaning of Your Idea

The *Meaning* of your Idea is the totality of your story, because the meaning of your story is *everything* to your readers.

The definition of Meaning from *Merriam-Webster*:

The thing one intends to convey, especially by language.

For the purposes of our brainstorming workshop, Meaning is:

- *Your* why, *your* reason, *your* What-if.
- Your cause, the root and branch of your purpose for writing your book.
- Your mission, your book's destination.
- The fun, the thrill, the fascination.

The Meaning of your Idea should be your reason for writing your book in the first place. Your passion for your Idea will become the roaring engine of your entire manuscript, and will keep you writing like the wind, from Chapter One to The Very End.

To harness all that fiery momentum, you first need to fully understand the beating heart of your personal relationship to your Idea. In order to be the invincible champion of your Idea, it's critical that you understand the reason you chose it and what makes that Idea important to you.

Our relationships to the world around us are created exclusively by our personal experiences, and forge our feelings about every aspect of our lives. Love, hate, jealousy, anger, pride, joy—feelings and emotions that are as fraught with romance and adventure as they are with danger and misfortune. Understanding how to use these in our stories is the most powerful weapon in a writer's arsenal.

THE ORIGINS OF MEANING

Whatever Meaning you discover about your Idea as you brainstorm, you'll find that emotion is at the heart of it, at the core of every relationship.

- Emotion is the fuel that connects your readers to your protagonist's heart and soul, that makes readers care for him and worry for his well-being.
- Emotion-packed conflict occurs when you test the relationships between your characters during your story.
- Emotion is the stakes in *every* story, be the author Tom Clancy, Julia Quinn, or Julia Child.
- Emotion fuels the risk in every story, puts our fears and worries on high alert.
- Emotion heightens our expectations and invests us in the outcomes of the story.
- Emotion is your hero's long-held, zealously-protected, wrong-headed misbelief about the way the world works. A misbelief that collides with an 'ah-ha' moment that allows him to finally face and overcome his demons and attain his story goal.

No matter how unsympathetic your protagonist's actions may be in their attempt to reach their story goal, our empathy for their anguish and frustration will make us cheer for them along their journey, follow them over, under, and through every obstacle, and celebrate their success at the end of the story. *Our* success. After all, aren't we the protagonist, the hero?

Whether you're writing a Western, a high fantasy, or romance, a memoir, thriller, or biography, a self-improvement book, a coffee-table book, or a cookbook, the most important relationship to establish is with your reader.

As you begin to explore your Idea for its most effective story-telling elements, remember that life and bestsellers are all about the relationships that enrich and complicate our lives.

- Boyfriends, girlfriends, spouses
- Mothers and daughters, fathers and sons
- Grandsons and grandmothers
- Close friends and colleagues, old friends, new friends,
- Sisters and cousins, aunts and uncles.
- Mentors, rivals, pets, leaders, teachers and students
- Employers and employees, commanders and soldiers
- Heroes and heroines, heroes and villains

Dynamic relationships defined and driven by the delicious complexities of compassion, affection, attachment, admiration, attraction, fondness, pleasure, devotion, reverence, worship, kindness, generosity, intimacy, friendship, companionship ... and love of all stripes.

I'm not saying this just because I'm a romance writer, but because *love* is, and always has been, literature's most powerful *meaning*, its eternal *why*, the basis for the most powerful what-ifs, the source of our most beloved stories:

- *Casablanca*, my favorite movie of all time, is a love story: romance and heroism, sacrifice and greed, friendships and unexpected allies.
- *To Kill a Mockingbird* is a story of love and honor.
- *Downton Abbey* is an elegant tapestry of love stories, romantic and familial.
- The *Twilight* series is the paranormal tale of Juliet and her Romeo.
- *Die Hard* is a love story, as are *Lethal Weapon*, *The Terminator*, and the entire Marvel franchise.
- *Pride and Prejudice* and *Game of Thrones*: both wildly differing stories in every possible way, except that both rely on dynamic relationships, love and loathing, devotion-betrayal, yearning-indifference.
- *The Hunger Games* is a many-faceted love story, with family at its heart.
- *Breaking Bad*, *The Walking Dead*, *The Sopranos*. The arcs of each of these enormously popular and often violent TV series are motivated at their foundations by relationships built upon love of family.
- The *Harry Potter* series is one long love story. Voldemort had it right—Love is Old Magic: *"His mother left upon him the traces of her sacrifice ... this is old magic, I should have remembered it, I was foolish to overlook it ..."*

None of these iconic and wildly diverse stories would be as universally cherished and massively popular without the emotional relationships at their very core. Emotions are the way we humans recognize, understand, and negotiate the meaning— the why—of life's experiences and the many relationships we forge throughout our lifetimes.

If you want to succeed in our highly competitive business of commercial storytelling, if you want to touch your readers and make them hungry for your books, your Idea must engage their hearts.

While you're brainstorming the Meaning of your Idea, ask yourself the following questions:

- Why *you*?
- Why this particular Idea?
- Why now?
- Why does the Idea speak to your heart, to your soul?
- Why and how does your Idea connect to your emotions?
- What elements of your Idea are the most compelling to you?
- Why do you want to explore that Idea?

Example from:
ONCE UPON a TREASURE HUNT

MY IDEA REMINDER

A Victorian folklorist struggles to have her research taken seriously among cynical academics.

BRAINSTORMING THE MEANING

Why did the battle between a Victorian folk scholar and her misogynistic colleagues make me angry enough to tell her story?

Story is the way we humans have always sorted out the world around us.

- The coming of the railroads meant that people could easily travel a distance from their homes, away from the storytellers.
- Grandpa and the village storyteller no longer had a captive audience who sat around the hearth every night and listened to their tales and legends, who then took them home and shared with the next generation.
- Losing the magic of storytelling would be an irreplaceable loss.
- Male-dominated colleges diminishing female scholars awakened my outrage for the under-represented.

I was struck by the realization of how dramatically the Industrial Revolution had threatened the very existence of folktales and the old ways.

I also admired the dedication of those who braved the ridicule of their peers and set out to collect these stories before the storytellers had all passed away.

BRAINSTORMING THE WHAT-IF

Remember that the most enduring stories ask a powerful and engaging What-if question. In this case:

- What if no one is around to hear and remember the unwritten stories?
- What if no one is left alive to learn the stories and repeat them after the storytellers pass away?
- What if the ancient and beloved folktales themselves are threatened with oblivion, or lost to neglect and indifference?

- What if the railroad brings about the death of village culture?
- What if the social sciences and the arts are the first to fall to the bean counters?

After I brainstormed my list of What-ifs, I chose the one that spoke to me with the most passion:

THE WORKING WHAT-IF

What if the ancient and beloved folk tales and rituals must be rescued from oblivion or lost to neglect and indifference?

For more examples, let's check in with our Volunteer Brainstormers who are eager to share their Meanings and What-ifs.

The Meaning & What-if Exercise
from Our Volunteer Brainstormers

Example 1
The Vanishing Cyclist

THE IDEA REMINDER:

A bicyclist enters a car tunnel and vanishes.

BRAINSTORMING THE MEANING:

Why did the incident of the vanishing cyclist intrigue the writer for such a long time?

During the workshop the writer's Idea seemed to really resonate with the other attendees who collectively brainstormed a slew of questions:

- Was it an accident? Hit and run? A kidnapping? A domestic violence incident? A revenge killing? An alien abduction? A CIA extraction? Did he disappear through a time warp? Or a disguised door leading into a top-secret laboratory?

- Were they an innocent caught in the crossfire between warring factions? Did they fake their own disappearance? To outrun the law, debts, divorce? A tryst in the tunnel?
- If the cyclist died in the tunnel, what happened to the body? Where are the police, the emergency vehicles, the accident investigators? Who found the body? Was the cyclist ever reported missing? Why not?
- Who was the cyclist? An unfaithful spouse? An assassin from the future? Wealthy? Homeless? A doctoral student at a nearby university bio lab? Are they famous? Infamous? A billionaire venture capitalist? A well-respected spiritual leader? A muck-raking politician?

Whew! Brainstorming on overdrive! Great fun! Great story questions! Too many, of course, but determining the best of them is what the process is all about.

For the writer, the brainstorming exercise helped clarify for her that the fate of the vanishing cyclist was the element that had sparked her imagination all those decades after the incident.

THE MEANING:

The writer's concern for the fate of the cyclist elicits fear for their safety, doubt, uneasiness, curiosity, apprehension, suspense, giving the original Idea the source of its Meaning, and providing a very powerful central engine.

BRAINSTORMING THE WHAT-IF:

From the Meaning, the writer brainstormed the What-if:

- What if the fate of the cyclist exposes a dangerous conspiracy?
- What if the fate of the cyclist reveals an illicit love affair?
- What if the fate of the cyclist was a plot contrived by the cyclist to vanish in order to escape a worse fate? A crime? Criminals?
- What if the fate of the cyclist goes viral after a social media post ignites a global search that puts the original poster in danger?

THE WORKING WHAT-IF:

What if the fate of the cyclist exposes a dangerous conspiracy?

Example 2
Library in the Woods

THE IDEA REMINDER:

A 24-hour lending library in the woods.

BRAINSTORMING THE MEANING:

Why did the Idea of the woodland library follow me so closely that I always included it as an example in my First Spark workshops?

- The librarian made me imagine an enchanting, twinkle-eyed elf who delighted in sharing her love of reading.
- Literacy is life, because our ability to communicate is everything that makes us human, and engages all of our senses: sight, touch, hearing, taste, smell, and that mystical sixth sense.

- The written word is our emotional connection to the past, the present, the future.
- Libraries are a repository of every human thought and experience.
- Folktales are often populated by mythical entities who live in a world of magic and enchantments. These entities take great pride in intersecting and interfering with human lives.

THE MEANING:

I loved the idea that whether library patrons arrived mid-day or in the middle of the night, they would find the windows aglow, the door unlocked, and a comfy chair, an open invitation for all to come read and browse and borrow. A truly magical setting.

The woods conjure mystical places, fey creatures, distorting sensations, misty creeks, shadows, stone, dappled sunlight, where mythical beings live and play, taunt and tease.

BRAINSTORMING THE WHAT-IF:

- What if the library is a safe house for the CIA?
- What if the library is a trysting place for a forbidden relationship?
- What if the librarian dies and her family wants to sell the property and close the library?
- What if the 24-hour lending library in the woods is a portal between the lands of fairy creatures and humans? (*An idea borrowed from an attendee at one of my bookstore workshops who emailed me afterward that she had used my woodland library idea for a paranormal short story.*)

THE WORKING WHAT-IF:

What if the 24-hour lending library in the woods is a portal between the lands of fairy creatures and humans?

Example 3
One Heiress Too Many

THE IDEA REMINDER:

Warehousing the inconvenient sons and daughters of the nobility in a chaotic household far from home.

BRAINSTORMING THE MEANING:

Why did the idea of warehousing inconvenient noble children stay with me over the years?

- I feel sorry for the hapless Catherine Howard, who was manipulated into a fatal marriage by her family, who used her as a pawn in their thirst for political power.
- Family connections are the foundation of life, our closest relationships are the source of who we become.
- In order for children to correctly understand who they are and where they fit in the world, they need to feel cherished, be assured they belong.
- The cruelty of politics. An unsupervised childhood without boundaries. A carelessly cruel husband. An uncaring family.

- A child who grows up in an environment of emotional scarcity will constantly seek a place to belong.
- Searching to create a family of the people in her small sphere, she would make friends and enemies: kind and dangerous, life-long and transient, BFFs and scheming rivals, nurturing and deceitful.
- Also, I am a long-time, unapologetic Anglophile.

THE MEANING:

Family is everything, especially to a child who needs the support of people who care about her needs.

BRAINSTORMING THE WHAT-IF

- What if she is the daughter of the king?
- What if this is an alternate universe, time-shifted?
- What if she has grown up wise and capable, despite the neglect of her family?
- What if she has learned a dangerous state secret?
- What if her powerful family loses its leader and she's evicted from the protection of the dower house?

THE WORKING WHAT-IF

What if the leader of a young woman's powerful family is executed for treason, leaving her to flee for her life, with nothing but her wits and a dangerous state secret?

Example 4
Diary of a Honeymoon

THE IDEA REMINDER:

The travel diary adventures of a young couple embarking on their marriage in a new century.

BRAINSTORMING THE MEANING:

Why did the idea of a travel diary about a young couple embarking on their marriage in a new century so enchant me?

- The bride's letters are a delightful glimpse into the beginning of the romantic early years of touring the highways and byways of the USA, the social mores of the times, and the early days of what I understand was a long and very happy marriage.
- Which also reminded me of the Lucy Ball and Desi Arnaz movie, *The Long, Long Trailer*, where the couple tows a huge travel trailer/honeymoon cottage across the country, hoping for a romantic journey but quickly discovering that love and marriage require compromise and forgiveness.
- Marriage is a journey of hills and valleys, spectacular vistas and comfy chairs, cliff-hangers and Elysian Fields.
- A honeymoon can be a magical time for a pair of newlyweds, a season of romance that holds reality at bay for a time.
- The exciting new century, the new technology, the honeymoon couple's new life together.
- The open road, expanding horizons.
- The early chapters of a marriage, forecasting the future, getting to know each other.

THE MEANING:

I love the idea of a newlywed bride documenting her honeymoon travels with her new husband, the ups and downs and sideways of the adventure of a lifetime.

Note: *This particular story idea can be told in a variety of ways:*

NON-FICTION:

- As a verbatim epistolary narration, chronological transcriptions of the letters, and/or images of the actual letters, accompanied by an editorial commentary on the couple's journey.
- A docu-diary, with a Point-of-View narrator, imagined dialog and conversations, citing portions of the letters and reactions to ephemera. This form allows for greater emotional engagement and connection with the reader than would a verbatim narration.

FICTION:

- As a novelist, I was instantly intrigued by the fictional possibilities inherent in the story of a young bride accompanying her groom on a months-long, cross-country business trip in the early days of automobile travel, where they are required to interact along the way with motel owners, small towns and big cities, roadside attractions, the new national park system, fellow travelers, road hazards, maintenance issues.

A COMBINATION OF FICTION AND NON-FICTION:

- Being a huge fan of vintage ephemera, I respond to both the monetary and emotional value of the collection.
- The basic idea of a cross-country honeymoon easily transports to any time period, past, present, future, into outer space, the jungle, set in the midst of unanticipated danger, the ocean, a wilderness, the Zombie Apocalypse, along the Oregon Trail ....

BRAINSTORMING THE WHAT-IF:

- What if the letters and memorabilia are published as a non-fiction record of an earlier time?
- What if possession of the collection is the center of a dispute between family members?
- What if the letters contain private or embarrassing truths about the couple or the company he works for?
- What if the bride stumbles across a crime or mystery that hounds their entire journey?
- What if the spoiled bride has to be convinced to leave the comfort of home to accompany her new husband on his trip?
- What if the honeymoon couple sets out on the Oregon Trail?

THE WORKING WHAT-IF

What if the honeymoon mirrors their journey: starts out full of promise, encounters obstacles that make them question the wisdom of marrying each other, before love blossoms again through their shared hardships.

As you begin to brainstorm the Meaning of the Idea you've chosen, keep in mind that all great story questions begin with a powerful and engaging What-if.

THE MEANING & WHAT-IF
~ BRAINSTORMING WORKSHEET ~

List as many elements as you can think of that give Meaning to your Idea.

Once you've got 10-20 meaningful elements, choose the one that touches you most deeply, then create a compelling What-if story question.

(Add, subtract, or change, as your understanding of the Meaning and What-if of your Idea evolves—which it will.)

BRAINSTORM YOUR MEANING:

BRAINSTORM YOUR WHAT-IF:

STEP 3
YOUR THEME WORDS

Theme!?! Ack! Nooo!

I hope I didn't make you cringe just now! Does that word fling you back into the dizzying boredom of high school English class like it does me?

Oh, how I hated the search for literary themes among the pages of some crusty old, classic, public domain novel. I rarely read the assigned book, so the in-class discussion always rocked me to sleep.

Yet, here I am, 50+ years later, recommending the subject myself, shocked to admit that Theme has become one of my BBFs —Best Brainstorming Friends.

Definitions of Theme from *Merriam-Webster* and Dictionary.com:

- *A subject or topic of discourse or of artistic representation*
- *A unifying or dominant idea, motif*

A bit of a dry mouthful, but, yeah, both definitions work for me in the context of storytelling.

THEME IN REAL LIFE

- If the theme of your high school grad night was Desire Under the Sea, your eager decorating committee probably festooned the hall with fishing nets, coral and kelp, boats, seagulls, seashells, tropical fish, sunken treasure, swaying palms, and little grass shacks. The prom activities surely included crowning a King Neptune and a Princess Ariel, depending on your generation, of course!
- The theme of our family home in the Oregon woods is Log Cabin Retreat. Our decor is replete with knotty pine paneling, a chain-saw bear sculpture, National Park memorabilia, a river stone fireplace, moose and squirrel, woodland bric-a-brac.
- Disneyland is the quintessential Theme Park, where spectacular vistas and enchanting motifs transport us from land to land. To Adventureland with the exotic sights and sounds of the Tiki Room, the river smells of the Jungle Cruise, music pouring from the Pirates of the Caribbean, each experience calling us to come inside, to join the fun, even to purchase a hat at the adventure-themed Bazaar!

THE MEANING OF THEME FOR WRITERS

Theme is an essential building block of your story world. It's the foundation of your plot and the clay with which you mold your characters. It reveals where they live and work, how they begin and end their journey, it's the place your readers will visit as they're reading your book.

- Theme is the underpinnings of your novel's emotion, usually visible, but always experienced by your readers.
- It's the poetry in your story question and the passion in your character's goals.
- The deeper the layers of theme, the stronger the emotional impact on your readers.
- Theme is the Technicolor lens through which your POV characters see and experience the world you create for them. It's how they approach every scene, every obstacle, every mentor, ally, and enemy.

Theme is the relationships between your Protagonist and:

- Their love interest, their boss, and colleagues
- Their family members, mom, dad, siblings
- Their friends, enemies, rivals, and detractors
- Their home, the kitchen, the fridge, their meals
- Their car, their desk, their yoga classmates
- Theme is the five senses of a character's thoughts and experiences
- Their goals and desires
- Their pride and their shame
- Their internal wounds, beliefs and misbeliefs
- Their successes and failures, professional and personal

As you can see, Theme can be an invaluable insight into a character's POV, which is your most useful tool for revealing their emotional landscape as they encounter obstacles along their journey.

Theme can also help you develop and express the character of your own writer's voice. Before I begin writing a single word of my novels, I brainstorm a list of POV theme words associated with the What-if.

Example from:
ONCE UPON a TREASURE HUNT

MY WHAT-IF REMINDER

What if the ancient and beloved folk tales and rituals must be rescued from oblivion, or lost to neglect and indifference?

EXAMPLE THEME WORDS BRAINSTORMING LIST

- Dragon, draco, worm, serpent, beast, brute, chimera, demon, heathen, monster, ogre, rascal, savage, scoundrel, villain, ruthless, cold-hearted, greedy.
- Sprite, elfin, invisible, furtive, apparition, archangel, phantom, fairy, dwarf, brownie, fay, gnome, leprechaun, nymph, pixie, siren, sylph, temptress, crafty.
- Air, wind, voice, melody, song, tune, storm, breeze, ambience, aura, breath, broadcast, charisma, charm, circulate, fly, soar, free, airy, light-hearted.
- Fire, blaze, burn, candle, conflagration, hearth, light, ardor, arouse, excite, fervor, firestorm, fuel, ignite, inferno, inflame, inspire, intensity, kindle, pitch, power.
- Hunt, pursue, probe, investigate, seek, inquiry, question, sift through, pry, delve, inspect, survey, review, scan, consider, appraise, quest, explore, dig.
- Faith, belief, folk tales, mystical, arcane, clandestine, covert, cryptic, enigma, hidden, veiled, obscure, riddle, secluded, stealthy, undercover, undisclosed …

Once you've brainstormed your own list of Theme Words we'll use them to develop your Premise in Step 4, and elsewhere in the *First*

Spark workshop, to remind you of the emotional origins of your Idea, and how that relates to your story.

I use my list as I create my characters, develop their POVs, shape their dialog, and construct their personal and public relationships. When I want to look at my story world through the eyes of my characters, I put my list of Theme Words to work. Using Theme Words also naturally adds the language of symbols to any story.

Writerly tools that come directly from brainstorming my Theme. Cool, eh?

In the narrative example below, you'll see the way I used those dragon/fairy POV theme words in the romantic "Meet Cute" in Chapter 1 of *Once Upon A Treasure Hunt*.

THE SETUP

Mairey (Protagonist,) the folklorist, sees mining baron Jack (Antagonist) as a rampaging dragon [local folk tale dragon named Balforge]. Jack sees Mairey as a fey creature, crafty and deceptive, as capricious as quicksilver.

FROM MAIREY'S THIRD PERSON POV

(I've <u>underlined</u> Mairey's POV Theme Words)

> "Have you any idea how long it's taken me to find you, Mairey Faelyn?"
> Mairey stared at the <u>shape in the doorway,</u> at the <u>dragon who knew her name.</u> Before she could demand to know

why or who he was, he was <u>bearing down on her</u> in a <u>gait
that thundered</u> across the planked floor.

But there she stood like a <u>stunned rabbit</u>, a thousand and
one questions knotted up inside her brain. She couldn't
move at all, and just when it seemed the <u>great beast would
overtake her</u>, he shifted his weight and <u>coursed around her</u>
in a <u>lingering circle</u>, brimming her lungs with <u>his startling
scent of bergamot and saddle-leather</u>, making her think
absurdly of Sir Thomas Browne's observation that <u>serpents
copulated in slow, sinuous spirals, length against languid
length, turning and turning against each other</u> ... just as
Mairey herself was doing with this <u>Balforge-incarnate</u>,
countering backward until she bumped against a post and
was forced to stare up into <u>his coal-dark eyes</u>.

Notice the thematic way that Mairey thinks of Jack in terms of
dragons and mining, and herself as his prey (a rabbit), sinuous
serpents, erotic scents, the sensuous advances of a predatory
dragon who knows her name. I chose each of these words and
phrases to elicit Mairey's fear and trepidation when this imposing
stranger comes looking for her.

You'll find a more extensive list of Theme Words for *Once Upon
A Treasure Hunt* in the Extended Theme Words section in the back
of this book.

Here's an additional example of the Theme Words and symbols I
used to develop the characters and plot for my medieval romance
The Maiden Bride: a Castle Keep Romance, set in the chaotic after-
math of the Black Death.

NOTE: *The terms below are part of my pre-writing notes only, not a part of the manuscript.*

Eleanor is a survivor, a medieval entrepreneur; a widow who creates family from the lost souls she encounters in her struggles to rebuild her dead husband's castle.
She is the gentle rain that falls onto the high, rocky slopes of a mountain top, a tiny rill that joins a stream as it begins to rush toward a cliff, eventually wearing down even the stoutest boulder, one drop at a time, until it breaks down and becomes the soil of the broad meadows and ripening fields below that great mountain, where the crops are soon ripening in the sunshine.

Nicholas is a powerful knight, brought to his knees by loss and guilt. Now a walking dead man, he believes himself God-forsaken, unredeemable; he's given up on life and society.
His heart has hardened to stone, and, like a mythical gargoyle, he haunts the tumbled ramparts of his own abandoned castle, driving away anyone who might attempt to soften him, especially his proxy-wed wife.

Symbolically, Eleanor represents the purity of water, an unstoppable force of nature that meets Nicholas' immovable objections, gently softening his gargoyle-self until his heart breaks free of his past and he can live in the world again.

The two examples above help demonstrate how understanding the thematic essence, the passions, at the heart of your idea will help you reveal the character types who will best populate your story.

As you brainstorm your list of Theme Words, be sure to explore all sides of your Idea's Theme, including:

- Positive words/phrases
- Negative words/phrases
- Character traits, emotions, motivations
- Opposites (e.g. Idealist v. Realist)
- Beliefs, truths, values, emotions
- Irony, cynicism, attitudes
- Nouns, verbs, adverbs, locations
- Desires, needs, expectations
- The five physical senses: sight, sound, smell, taste, touch
- The paranormal senses

As your list of Theme Words grows, you'll begin to sense those words that resonate with you and with your original Idea. Flag these. They are the sparks you're looking for as you go forward with your story.

Theme ought to run deeply through your story, and can be a great help in staying on track, and making sure that characters remain true to themselves and thereby to your story.

And in these very early stages of writing, brainstorming your list of Theme Words can help pinpoint what excites your senses and your heart about the Meaning of the Idea you chose.

It's time to look in on our Volunteer Brainstormers and their lists of Theme Words.

THE THEME WORDS EXERCISE
FROM OUR VOLUNTEER BRAINSTORMERS

Example 1
The Vanishing Cyclist

WHAT-IF REMINDER:

What if the fate of the cyclist exposes a dangerous conspiracy?

BRAINSTORMING THEME WORDS

- Dangerous, cover up, occult, suspected, unmarked, vanished, dark, camouflaged, truth, fragile, cloak-and-dagger, spy, genius, mysterious, enemy, illusion.
- Premonition, nameless, classified, shadowy, apprehensive, fate, expectation, undercover, conspiracy, overlooked, flight, sinister, pursue, fearless, betrayal.
- Threat, threaten, underground, fear, foreshadow, suspicion, clandestine, unknown, forewarn, ambush, covert, unseen, hope, portent, assault, trap, innocence, hunch.

- Prediction, foresee, dread, prophecy, waylay, mole, operative, traitor, malevolence, entrap, agent, patriot, inhospitable, set trap, courage, reckless, competition.
- Deception, hit and run, violence, missing, surprise, accident, kidnap, revenge, athletic, brutal, secret, hidden, lone, future, past, destiny, heroic, vulnerable.

Example 2
Library in the Woods

WHAT-IF REMINDER:

What if the 24-hour lending library in the woods is the portal between the lands of fairy creatures and humans?

BRAINSTORMING THEME WORDS:

- Enchantment, darkness, books, repository, shadowy, literacy, mystical, secrets, unexpected, welcoming, wonder, fairy tale, liberty, woodland, illiterate, library.
- Folklore, forest, oak, pine, fir, nighthawk, lending, otherworldly, deer, understory, owls, endow, squirrels, misty, borrow, beguile, belonging, magical, witchery.
- Spells, ensorcell, sorcery, bewitch, wizard, ancient, leafy glade, wildfire, smokey, campfire, charm, belief, escape, sprite, mysterious, portal, gateway, fable, spirit.
- Legend, myth, ghost, forbidden, mushrooms, forsake, ancient, arcane, fish out of water, between worlds, storyteller, stories, wicked, stepmother, maleficent, evil.
- Evildoing, goodness, kindness, virtue, generosity, grace, merciless, beauty, beast, monster, ogre, merciful, destiny, karma, purpose, make believe, love, malignant.

Example 3
One Heiress Too Many

WHAT-IF REMINDER:

What if the leader of a young woman's powerful family is executed for treason, leaving her to flee for her life, with nothing but her wits and a dangerous state secret?

BRAINSTORMING THEME WORDS:

- Lonely, secrets, danger, scholarly, politics, fate, destiny, birthright, powerful, belonging, scarcity, deceit, treachery, conspiracy, mystery, abundance, neglect.
- Devious, undependable, shady, faithless, fickle, alchemy, loyalty, kinship, acceptance, potential, influence, privilege, sovereignty, domination, baseborn.
- Dominion, prerogative, inheritance, legacy, charade, occult, oracle, tainted, isolation, resilience, covert, clandestine, stealth, oppression, adversary, guardian.
- Oppression, privacy, marriage, expedient, avarice, fortune, legacy, title, nobility, greed, desire, love, mistrust, scandal, legitimate, illegitimate, justice, benevolent.
- Grandiosity, masquerade, outlaw, family, heir, kindred, friends, honor, dignity, trust, deference, fealty, homage, obeisance, rank, reputation, pride, courage.

Example 4
Diary of a Honeymoon

WHAT-IF REMINDER:

What if the honeymoon mirrors their journey: starts out full of promise, encounters obstacles that make them question the wisdom of marrying each other, before love blossoms again through their shared hardships?

BRAINSTORMING THEME WORDS:

- Honeymoon, memories, family, adventure, outreach, lovers, letters, cross-country, automobile, romance, journey, compromise, forgiveness, embarking, mapping.
- Diary, surprises, love, friendship, homesick, marriage, bride, groom, diary, legacy, travel, breakdown, hospitality, welcome, junket, progress, sightseeing, traverse.
- Share, experience, demanding, exhausting, stormy, regret, whining, tourist trap, explore, remote, frontier, pioneer, backwoods, broken-down, lonely, unexpected.
- Accident, accidental, amazing, unforeseen, excursion, rubberneck, vintage, insight, perception, adjustment, impression, empathy, ignorance, diversity, prejudice.
- Attitude, journal, observation, destination, happily ever after, relationship, promise, expansive, roadway, wedding, honeymoon, alliance, conjugal, majestic, assumption.

Now it's time to brainstorm your own list of Theme Words!

Your Theme Words
~ Brainstorming Worksheet ~

With your Meaning and What-if in mind from Step 2, list single words, simple terms, or phrases you associate with your original Idea in Step 1.

Take your time. No rush. Brainstorm alone or with your writers group, or your family. Leave the exercise for a few days, then add more words as you think of them. List words, terms and phrases, positives & negatives. Dig into a thesaurus, one of my favorite places to discover Theme Words.

Don't analyze. No judgment. No right or wrong. No holds barred.

Brainstorm Your Theme Words!

Ack, *Premise!* Yet another literary device-of-the-devil I feared and resented in high school! I mean, why did a 17-year-old Southern California girl in the late 1960s need to read *Silas* (oh, yawn ...) *Marner*, let alone seek out and understand its premise?

And yet, here I am, all those years later, proudly proclaiming the once-annoying Premise as another of my BBFs.

The *Merriam-Webster* definition of premise:

A proposition antecedently supposed or proved as a basis of argument or inference specifically, something assumed or taken for granted: presupposition.

Simply, Premise is the point you want to prove. It's the foundation of your story, a universal truth told in the briefest, most straightforward terms. A premise is *not* a short logline, which is a brief summary of a story, complete with main character and hinting at the plot.

Logline example of *Star Wars:*

A restless farm boy joins rebel forces to save the galaxy from an evil empire.

Too many story details for the purposes of our Step 4 Premise. We're not there yet, but we'll get there in Step 6 with the Elevator Pitch, after we brainstorm the critical Story Elements.

In the meantime:

- A story Premise has three parts, representing Character A, Character B and the Action (Part C).
- One of your characters will be driven to act out the A Part of your Premise.
- The opposing character or force will act out the B Part of the Premise.

Which gives your story two Characters who will operate in direct opposition to each other, ensuring that your story has an organically powerful conflict.

The Action (Part C) of your story represents the essence of that conflict.

- Think of the Action (C) as the journey *from* a situation – > *to* a different situation. The action verb provides the direction and mode of the story arc and activates the story question.

Of course, a Premise is not a story in itself.

Think of the Premise as the promise you make to your readers that your characters and their struggles along their journey will have meaning in the end by proving the message at the heart of your story.

The most exciting thing about developing a Premise *before* you begin banging away on your keyboard is that you'll know up front the types of Characters you'll need to develop as well as the Actions they must take in order to support your Premise.

Let's say my list of brainstormed Theme Words includes the following:

- Unconditional love, betrayal, self-respect, sharing, caring, honorable, heroic, chaos, vulgar, worthless, the present, the past, victory, terror, neglect, goodness, charlatan, charm, dramatic, compassion, peace, love, truth, lies.

To develop my Premise, I brainstorm sets of Theme Words that represent the opposing characters (A & B Premise Actors) who will tell the opposing sides of my story Idea:

- Unconditional love/betrayal
- Victory/terror, fear
- Compassion/self-respect
- The past/the present
- Personal courage/public censorship

Then I add one of the go-to Action Words (C) from my list:

- Conquers, destroys, risks, leads to ….

Examples of these brainstormed combinations:

- Unconditional love (A) *conquers* (C) betrayal (B).
- Betrayal (B) *destroys* (C) unconditional love (A) .
- Personal courage (A) *risks* (C) public censorship (B).
- Self-respect (A) *leads to* (C) compassion for others (B).
- The easiest victory (A) *is won by* (C) terror and fear (B).
- Honor the past (A) *by living* (C) in the present (B).

A PREMISE CAN ALSO INCLUDE A PAIR OF CLAUSES

- To find (C) good in oneself (A), we must look for it (C) first in others (B).
- It's impossible to hold fast (C) to the old (A) while reaching out for (C) the new (B).
- The cost (C) of endless attention to business (A) is the endless neglect (C) of many other things (B).

BRAINSTORM YOUR PREMISE

Start by reviewing your list of Theme Words.

- Flag those that are the most intensely, emotionally relevant to how your Idea makes you feel, how your story relates to those feelings, and the message you want your readers to experience.
- Add more words when they occur to you. Use whatever comes to you in your brainstorming moments.

At this point it also helps if you know the general trajectory of your story, such as:

- <u>Positive</u>: from doubt to hope; from subjugation to freedom.
- <u>Negative</u>: from hope to doubt; from freedom to subjugation.

Example from:
ONCE UPON a
TREASURE HUNT

THE WHAT-IF REMINDER

What if the ancient and beloved folk tales and rituals must be rescued from oblivion, or lost to neglect and indifference?

To create my Premise for *Once Upon A Treasure Hunt*, I referred back to my What-if as well as the Theme Words list I brainstormed in Step 3.

- *Fairy, dragon, cold-hearted, ruthless, sprite, hearth, heart, inferno, naive, savage, charm, powerful, hunt, quest, mystical, secrets, ancient, vows, love.*

BRAINSTORMING MY PREMISE

- A family secret leads to jealous greed.
- A generous heart invites betrayal.
- Fearless determination overwhelms the most ruthless hunter.
- … and many others.

MY WORKING PREMISE

Faith in the human heart overcomes the coldest reality.

Crafting your Premise is a chance to explore your Idea for all the amazing places it can take your story, and all the fascinating Characters who can drive your story to its destination.

BRAINSTORMING ADDITIONAL ACTION (C) WORDS

- Begets, generates, brings, produces, begins, reveals, brings forth, causes, compels, demands, drives, imposes, inflicts, limits, obliges, pressures, requires, forces.
- Always, never, forever, repeatedly, keeps, routinely, generally, reverses, removes, concludes, contains, settles, induces, governs, controls, imposes, commands.
- Opens, closes, drives away, alters, diminishes, evolves, modifies, reduces, reforms, resolves, transforms, adapts, warps, unravels, tangles, breaks.
- Solves, provokes, changes, makes, exposes, gives, crushes, routs, trumps, resolves, foments, incites, offends, raises, clarifies, determines, explains.
- Start your own Action Word list and keep adding to it as words come to you. Store it in your writer's toolbox for future projects. After all, stories always need Action and Action guarantees Conflict.

Time to see how our Volunteer Brainstormers are doing with their Premises.

THE PREMISE EXERCISE
FROM OUR VOLUNTEER BRAINSTORMERS

Note: *For the lists of the Theme Words associated with the examples below, refer back to their Theme Word Examples in Step 3.*

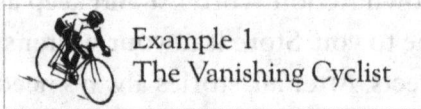
Example 1
The Vanishing Cyclist

WHAT-IF REMINDER:

What if the fate of the cyclist exposes a dangerous conspiracy?

BRAINSTORMING POSSIBLE PREMISES:

- Uncompromising defiance in the face of impossible odds overcomes the fiercest enemy. (Positive trajectory)
- A fearless heart exposes the coldest conspiracy. (Positive trajectory)
- A reckless past leads to a sinister future. (Negative trajectory)
- A baffling mystery leads to death.
- A baffling mystery leads to forbidden love.

- An everyday activity cloaks a horrific truth.

THE WORKING PREMISE:

Uncompromising defiance in the face of impossible odds overcomes the fiercest enemy.

> Example 2
> Library in the Woods

WHAT-IF REMINDER:

What if the 24-hour lending library in the woods is a portal between the lands of fairy creatures and humans?

BRAINSTORMING POSSIBLE PREMISES:

- An open heart invites goodness and light, a closed one only shadows.
- Evil enchants the strong as easily as the weak.
- The power of love is as ancient as wickedness.
- A welcoming library can open a closed mind and fill an empty heart.

THE WORKING PREMISE:

A free and welcoming library can open a closed mind and fill an empty heart.

> Example 3
> One Heiress Too Many

WHAT IF REMINDER:

What if the leader of a young woman's powerful family is executed for treason, leaving her to flee for her life, with nothing but her wits and a dangerous state secret?

BRAINSTORMING POSSIBLE PREMISES:

- A noble heart can uplift the most villainous scoundrel.
- Steadfast courage vanquishes scandal and treachery.
- Destiny is a living thing, not anchored in history.
- A noble heart can turn destiny from scarcity to abundance.
- A forgiving heart can turn scarcity to abundance.
- Own your character, own your destiny.

THE WORKING PREMISE:

An open and forgiving heart can turn scarcity to abundance.

Example 4
Diary of a Honeymoon

WHAT IF REMINDER:

What if the honeymoon mirrors their journey: starts out full of promise, encounters obstacles that make them question the wisdom of marrying each other, before love blossoms again through their shared hardships?

BRAINSTORMING POSSIBLE PREMISES:

- A journey of 5,000 miles begins with the first step.
- Marriage is the most difficult journey of all.
- Life is a journey, not a destination.
- Marriage is a journey, not a destination.
- A marriage of a lifetime begins on the first day.

THE WORKING PREMISE:

Marriage is a journey, not a destination.

Whoop! It's your turn to brainstorm your Premise.

Reminder: Don't restrict your choice to your Theme Word list; just grab whatever words or phrases feel right to you and to your story Idea.

YOUR PREMISE
~ **BRAINSTORMING WORKSHEET** ~

PREMISE TEMPLATE:

- One of your characters will be driven to act out the A Part of your Premise.
- The opposing character or force will act out the B Part of the Premise.
- The Action (Part C) of your story represents the essence of the conflict.

BRAINSTORM YOUR PREMISE:

YOUR WORKING PREMISE:

STEP 5
YOUR CHARACTERS

At last! My favorite part of crafting a story! Meeting and getting to know my characters! And the best way to get to know them is to force them into a fiery conflict that's guaranteed to reveal their essences.

Conflict is the basis for every story.
Character is the basis for every conflict.

Conflict must spring organically from unrelenting opposition to your main characters' goals and motivations, beliefs and misbeliefs, strengths and weaknesses.

My guess is that even while you were brainstorming your Premise in Step 4, a noisy mob of characters began shouting for your attention.

"Pick me! Hey, author! Over here!"

You might already have a few specific characters in mind to help tell your story. Orchestrating their motives and actions in opposition to each other is critical to building the arc of their journey.

Whether a major or minor character in your story, each has a single job to do: to act out your Premise according to their job description.

PROTAGONIST'S (A) JOB DESCRIPTION

- To show, explore, and ruthlessly defend Part A of the Premise.
- The Protagonist can be a combination of your brainstormed character types.

ANTAGONIST'S (B) JOB DESCRIPTION

- To show, explore, and ruthlessly defend Part B of the Premise.
- The Antagonist can be a combination of your brainstormed character types.

AUTHOR'S (C) JOB DESCRIPTION

- To provide a crucible for Part C of the Premise, the Action verb.
- A literary crucible is an inescapable situation that none of the characters can avoid by simply walking away or deciding not to care.
- Though you've already decided on the Action part of your Premise, this exercise is invaluable for brainstorming thematically relevant obstacles you can use to impede the Protagonist's progress while writing the story.

CHARACTERS IN OPPOSITION

One of the most effective ways to increase the power of your story, is to orchestrate your main characters in direct opposition to each other and their goals.

The best way to create that dynamic is for your Protagonist's greatest strength to also be their greatest weakness.

If the Protagonist struggles to reconcile their greatest strength with her greatest weakness, then during her journey she must not only do battle against the Antagonist to reach her goal, but against herself and her own world view.

EXAMPLES OF CHARACTER TRAITS IN OPPOSITION

(adapted from *The Art of Dramatic Writing*, by Lajos Egri)

- Brave – Cowardly
- Joyful – Solemn
- Clever – Dull
- Peaceful – Violent
- Happy – Morbid
- Naive – Worldly
- Optimist – Pessimist
- Neat – Messy
- Faithful – Faithless
- Loyal – Cheating

GREATEST STRENGTH/ GREATEST WEAKNESS

Our greatest personal strength as humans can often be our greatest weakness, and is bound to wreak havoc with our goals.

A personal example in my writing life: I'm a great researcher! I can spend days digging up the tiniest, fluffiest bit of unnecessary historical detail, when I should actually be writing the next two chapters!

Orchestrating the strength and weakness of the Protagonist in direct opposition to the Antagonist's heightens the dramatic action of the Premise, not only as they pursue their opposing story goals, but as they struggle against each other's most basic impulses.

Properly orchestrated, these Characters will launch the conflict with such momentum that the middle of the story can't possibly sag.

PROTAGONIST EXAMPLES

Greatest strength: Loyal
Greatest weakness: Blindly loyal

Greatest strength: Generous
Greatest weakness: Overly generous

ANTAGONIST EXAMPLES

Greatest strength: Driven to succeed
Greatest weakness: Target hypnosis

Greatest strength: Assertive
Greatest weakness: Contravenes authority

BRAINSTORM YOUR CHARACTERS

Let's brainstorm a few Character types using two Examples from Step 5:

Unconditional love (A) *conquers* (C) betrayal (B).

(A) – Long-suffering spouse, parent, best friend, teacher, mentor.
    (C) – *Conquers* (Obstacles: death of a family member, unkept promises, disrespect, mistrust, shame, revelation, illness, accident, revenge, reversals.)
    (B) – Unfaithful spouse, abandoned family, lost soul.

Personal courage (A) *risks* (C) public censorship (B).

(A) – Politician, teacher, police officer, social media influencer, famous actor, author, religious leader, sports figure, whistle-blower.

(C) – *Risks* (Obstacles: News story, conspiracy, blackmail, truth, lies, divorce, scandal, affair, money laundering, cover-up, election loss.)

(B) – Rival politician, vengeful reviewer, powerful CEO, blackmailer, news reporter, false accuser, slum lord, corrupt investigator.

As you brainstorm your Characters from your existing Premise, remember to refer back to your fabulous list of Theme Words to help identify the best traits and qualities of your Protagonist and Antagonist, as well as the Obstacles that will reveal the Action.

Example from:
ONCE UPON a TREASURE HUNT

MY PREMISE REMINDER

Faith in the human heart overcomes the coldest reality.

BRAINSTORMING THE THREE PARTS OF MY PREMISE

Protagonist (A): *Faith in the human heart ...*

- Victorian college professor, archeologist, recent widow, research librarian, governess, tutor, museum director, writer, housekeeper, lady's maid, companion.

Action (C): *... overcomes ... (thematic story obstacles)*

- Secrets, plunder, enchant, yearn for, honor a pledge, conundrum, riddle, theft, compassion, intimacy, impasse, dilemma, arrogance, pride.

Antagonist (B): *... the coldest reality.*

- Ruthless landlord, corrupt judge, Member of Parliament, mining baron, dragon-heart, banker, rival archeologist, rival college professor, ancient secret society.

BRAINSTORMING MY POSSIBLE CHARACTERS

Protagonist's (A) Job Description: To show, explore, and ruthlessly defend *faith in the human heart ...*

In *Once Upon A Treasure Hunt*, 'faith in the human heart' is Mairey's defining characteristic. Everything she does, says and thinks will be slanted toward her part of the premise.

She believes in the goodness of people and has faith that they mean well, including the Antagonist, which is not only her greatest strength, but it also serves the dual role of being her greatest weakness, because she is too trusting at times, a trait that eventually threatens not only her safety, but the security of the Antagonist's world.

Antagonist's (B) Job Description: To show, explore, and ruthlessly defend *the coldest reality ...*

'The coldest reality' is Jack's defining characteristic and stands in direct opposition to Mairey's 'faith in the human heart,' putting the two of them at loggerheads from the start.

Jack thinks and acts in terms of reality and cold facts, is suspicious of people's motives, and fears the faith and goodness offered by the Protagonist. His ruthless pursuit of his goals is both his strength and weakness, making him a wildly successful mining baron, but unable to acknowledge the lodestar that would lead to a treasure far more precious than gold.

Author's (C) Job Description: To provide a crucible for the action verb … *overcomes* ….

For Mairey and Jack, that crucible [the race to reach the Willow-moon Knot first] contained the journey from mutual mistrust, to respect, to—because this is a romance—unconditional love. And I'm delighted to say that the outcome of their conflict proved the Premise I constructed from the Spark of my Idea, that 'faith in the human heart overcomes the coldest reality.'

Time to meet the Characters brainstormed by our plucky Volunteers.

THE CHARACTER EXERCISE
FROM OUR VOLUNTEER BRAINSTORMERS

Example 1
The Vanishing Cyclist

THE WORKING PREMISE REMINDER

Uncompromising defiance in the face of impossible odds overcomes the fiercest enemy.

BRAINSTORMING THE THREE PARTS OF THE PREMISE

Protagonist (A) *Uncompromising defiance in the face of impossible odds ...*

- Amateur sleuth, cyclist's sister, mother, ex-Marine cop, burned-out detective, group of misfit kids, the cyclist's cycling group, local FBI agent, cyclist's laboratory colleagues, cyclist's trainer, cyclist's spouse, lover, underappreciated newscaster.

Action (C) ... *overcomes* ...(multiple story obstacles that reflect the premise)

- Corruption, apathy, rivalry, red tape, inexperience, malfeasance, immorality, infamy, secret cipher, zealousness, cover up.

Antagonist (B) ... *the fiercest enemy.*

- Rogue military group, rival cycling group, local police department, foreign terrorists, global cabal of scientists, cartel, industrial espionage, Olympic team rival, cyclist's trainer, rogue government agency, vengeful lover, murderous spouse.

BRAINSTORMED CHARACTERS IN OPPOSITION

Protagonist (A):

The cyclist's sister is an ex-Marine, local FBI agent, and a member of her brother's cycling club.

Antagonist (B):

A rogue government agency in league with a cabal of mad scientists.

> Example 2
> Library in the Woods

THE WORKING PREMISE REMINDER

A free and welcoming library can open a closed mind and fill an empty heart.

BRAINSTORMING THE THREE PARTS OF THE PREMISE:

Protagonist (A) *A free and welcoming library ...*

- Fey librarian , firefighter, reluctant heir, forest ranger, retired teacher, librarian, fantasy author, logger, children, camper, book club member, ghost writer.

Action (C) *... can open ...* (multiple story obstacles that reflect the premise)

- Belief, misbelief, non-believer, fear, prejudice, greed, illiteracy, intolerance, injustice, xenophobia, disdain, apartheid.

Antagonist (B) *... a closed mind and fill an empty heart.*

- Tourist board, logging company, inheritors, evil witch/wizard, warring fairy tribes, national park status, mundane fairy hunters, hunters, school board, county library system, church leaders, local courts.

BRAINSTORMED CHARACTERS IN OPPOSITION

Protagonist (A):

- A forest ranger inherits a woodland library from her fey grandmother who started the book club fifty years before.

Antagonist (B)

- A local tourist board of mundane fairy hunters in league with the leader of an evil fairy tribe.

> Example 3
> One Heiress Too Many

THE WORKING PREMISE REMINDER:

An open and forgiving heart can turn scarcity to abundance.

BRAINSTORMING THE THREE PARTS OF THE PREMISE:

Protagonist (A) *An open and forgiving heart ...*

- Royal bastard, young widow, daughter of a noble family, abandoned orphan, rebellious bride, nun/postulant, tutor, disguised heiress, fugitive heiress, cut-purse, burglar, leader of a theft ring, alchemist, teacher.

Action (C) *... can turn ...* (multiple story obstacles that reflect the premise)

- Mistrust, pride, grandiosity, stealth, avarice, consent, control, arrest writ, imprisonment, illness, scandal, proclamation, exposed.

Antagonist (B) ... *scarcity to abundance.*

- The king, a rival, wicked relative, evil chamberlain, stepparent, chancery, a court rival, high sheriff, mother-in-law, half-sibling, rival guardians, evil bridegroom, false-hearted friend, bounty hunter.

BRAINSTORMED CHARACTERS IN OPPOSITION:

Protagonist (A):

The fugitive daughter of a treasonous noble hides from the king's minions by posing as an alchemist in the home of the high sheriff.

Antagonist (B):

An evil chamberlain and the heiress's cruel stepfather are vying for her valuable wardship.

Example 4
Diary of a Honeymoon

THE WORKING PREMISE REMINDER:

Marriage is a journey, not a destination.

BRAINSTORMING THE THREE PARTS OF THE PREMISE:

Protagonist (A) *Marriage ...*

(Since the Protagonist is a Bride, our Volunteer brainstormed personality traits.)

- Reluctant, complaining, homebody, resistant, spoiled, adventurous, sheltered, bold, unafraid, reckless, modest, intrepid, showy, daddy's girl, rich.

Action (C) ... *is a journey* ... (multiple story obstacles that reflect the premise)

- No vacancy, road hazards, bad food, miscommunication, weather, hunger, flat tire, car camping, exhaustion, getting lost, theft, first argument.

Antagonist (B) ... *not a destination.*

(The Antagonists in this case are the Bride's expectations and the Cross-Country trip itself.)

- Long hours on road, new husband, husband distracted, husband inattentive, road map, competing hotels, diner food quality, the clock/time, mean hotel manager, tour guide, small town police, husband's home office, the unknown.

BRAINSTORMED CHARACTERS IN OPPOSITION:

Protagonist (A):

- A spoiled bride from a wealthy family accompanies her groom on a grueling cross-country trip in the 1920s.

Antagonist (B) *(Expectations and the trip itself)*

- Groom inattentive, distracted by road hazards, hotel managers, corrupt sheriff, fleas, and an unhappy bride.

Now it's time to brainstorm your cast of Characters, so you can
send them out into your Story World.

Your Characters
~ Brainstorming Worksheet ~

- Refer to your Theme Words as you brainstorm a list of Protagonists who might represent the (A) side of your premise.
- Brainstorm the same for possible Antagonists (B).
- Use the Action (C) column to brainstorm a list of thematic obstacles that will confound and impede your characters during the course of their journey.

PROTAGONIST–THE A PART OF YOUR PREMISE:

THE ACTION–THE C PART OF YOUR PREMISE:

ANTAGONIST–THE B PART OF YOUR PREMISE:

STEP 6
YOUR ELEVATOR PITCH

"What's your book about?"

Back in Step 1 we dealt with how to answer the awkward "Where do you get your ideas?" question. With a solid Elevator Pitch you can easily answer the most important question: "What's your book about?"

An Elevator Pitch is the brief story question you'll develop using all the elements you've brainstormed so far: your Idea, Meaning, Theme Words, Premise, and Characters.

The definition from AuthorMedia.com:

> *An elevator pitch is a way to quickly tell someone about your book in a way that makes them want to buy it.*

By this time, your story is probably beginning to follow you everywhere.

- You can feel it surging through the marrow of your writerly bones.
- Your fingers are itching to get to your keyboard.

- Your scenes and settings are obscuring the rest of the world, and your characters have taken up residence in your every thought.

Excellent news! Your story journey with your characters is just around the corner!

THE STORY ELEMENTS

The Elevator Pitch needs to be:

- No more than 2-3 sentences
- No longer than 30-60 seconds
- Fresh, sassy, provocative, irresistible, and dramatic

And include the major elements of your story, including your
...

- **Protagonist:** The Character who will prove Part A of your story Premise.
- **Situation:** The setup of your original Idea and its Meaning.
- **Inciting Incident:** The catalyst, how and why the Action begins.
- **Objective/Stakes:** The story goal, hints at obstacles and risks to Protagonist.
- **Antagonist:** The opposition, the Part B of your story Premise.
- **Central Conflict:** The Protagonist's desire collides with the Antagonist/Opposition. Asks the story question: Will the Protagonist succeed or fall to the power of the Antagonist?

In the final exercise of our workshop, we'll brainstorm these

Story Elements to incorporate into your endlessly handy Elevator Pitch.

Handy, because you can use your Pitch in dozens of effective ways:

- As the road map to your story.
- To show you where you are while on your story journey.
- To show you where you've been.
- To remind you where you're going.
- Your marketing hook, your newsletter headline.
- The blurb on the back of your print book.
- The header on your social media platforms.
- The book description on your retailer pages.
- A personal introduction to you and your voice.
- A quick promotional opportunity.
- The basis for the synopsis/outline of your story as you begin crafting your bestseller.

And, of course, your Elevator Pitch is the ultimate answer to the "What's your book about?" question, whether asked by an agent, an acquiring editor, a reviewer, a potential reader, your biggest fan, or even your favorite aunt's creepy boyfriend.

Your Elevator Pitch should be bold and beguiling. Here's the chance to use all of the elements you've brainstormed to conjure your most dramatic, hyperbolic–appropriate prose to:

Use your biggest, juiciest, most spectacular descriptions to enchant us with your characters and their perilous journey.

Make your pitch original, dazzling, timely, irresistible to everyone who reads or hears it.

Transform your once simple Idea into a brilliant, intensely hued extravaganza, guaranteed to amaze, amuse, and intrigue readers, editors, and reviewers.

Make them all say "Tell me more."

Strike the spark that will ignite your own passion for your Idea and your Characters, and illuminate your journey from Chapter 1 through The End.

Example from:
ONCE UPON a TREASURE HUNT

BRAINSTORMING MY ELEVATOR PITCH

To structure my Elevator Pitch for *Once Upon A Treasure Hunt*, I filled in the Story Elements from my Step 5 Characters in Opposition exercise.

- *Protagonist:* A young Victorian scholar ...
- *Situation:* ... who inherits her father's extensive folklore collection, and vows to protect the family's ancient secret.
- *Inciting Incident*: A rapacious mining baron confiscates her collection and demands she assist with his search for the ancient artifact she has vowed to protect with her life.
- *Objective/ Stakes:* In order to protect her family and its secret, she must stall and misdirect the baron on his quest.
- *Antagonist/ Opposition:* Discovering the man's warmth and goodness tests her beliefs; falling in love with him becomes an irresistible force that threatens to expose her secret.
- *Central Conflict:* Will she be able to protect her family's ancient secret from the baron before he can steal it, along with her heart?

After completing the Story Element exercise, I then sorted,

shuffled and condensed the text into the Logline and the Elevator Pitch you'll see below.

An Elevator Pitch comes in many sizes, from a seven-word Logline, to a full paragraph, to every length and complexity in-between, each created for a different use in a different situation. Below are my examples of two of the most useful pitches.

The Logline for *Once Upon A Treasure Hunt* uses the Protagonist (A) — Action (C) — Antagonist (B) parts of my Premise as the basic template: *Faith in the human heart overcomes the coldest reality.*

The Logline:
   A young woman (A) must protect her family's ancient secret (C) from a rapacious mining baron (B).

The Elevator Pitch includes the simple Premise, expanding on the Logline, while incorporating more detailed story elements.

The Elevator Pitch:
   A rapacious mining baron (B) demands (C) that a young woman (A) assist him in his search for an ancient artifact that will lead him to a legendary vein of silver—the very artifact she has vowed to safeguard with her life. Will she be able to protect her family's ancient secret from the baron before he can steal it, along with her heart?

Let's go see how our Volunteer Brainstormers have fared crafting their own Elevator Pitches.

THE ELEVATOR PITCH EXERCISE
FROM OUR VOLUNTEER BRAINSTORMERS

Example 1
The Vanishing Cyclist

THE STORY ELEMENTS:

- *Protagonist:* The missing cyclist's sister ...
- *Situation:* ... is an ex-Marine, local FBI agent, and a member of her brother's competition cycling group.
- *Inciting Incident:* He goes missing after entering a remote car tunnel and hasn't been seen since. When the authorities refuse to investigate ...
- *Objective/ Stakes:* ... she vows to find her brother, no matter that it may cost her job or her life.
- *Antagonist/ Opposition :* Her investigation exposes a rogue government agency in league with a cabal of mad scientists who are threatening the world.

- *Central Conflict:* Will the missing cyclist's sister discover the fate of her brother in time to bring down the powerful enemy and save the world?

THE LOGLINE:

A young woman's search for her brother exposes a global conspiracy and awakens the wrath of a powerful enemy.

THE ELEVATOR PITCH:

When the authorities refuse to investigate her brother's disappearance during a cycling event, a young FBI agent risks everything to find him and expose those responsible. Will she discover the fate of her brother in time to bring down the powerful enemy and save the world?

Example 2
Library in the Woods

THE STORY ELEMENTS

- *Protagonist:* An idealistic young forest ranger who enjoys isolation ...
- *Situation:* ... inherits a woodland library from her fey librarian grandmother.
- *Inciting Incident:* Her siblings threaten her claim to the library, revealing plans to tear it down and clearcut the woodland.
- *Objective/ Stakes:* To save the library and the forest from destruction and expose the wicked plot ...

- *Antagonist/ Opposition:* ... set in motion by the local tourist board of mundane fairy hunters who are in league with the leader of an evil fairy tribe.
- *Central Conflict:* Can the young ranger muster a large enough cohort of fey and human assistance to rout their enemy, rescue the library and the woodland, and restore peace to the forest?

THE LOGLINE:

Can a young woman rescue her enchanted woodland library before it can be destroyed by an evil, otherworldly rival?

THE ELEVATOR PITCH:

An idealistic young forest ranger inherits a woodland library from her fey librarian grandmother. With the backing of the leader of an evil fairy tribe, her siblings dispute her claim, threatening to destroy the library and clearcut the woodland. Will the ranger muster a large enough cohort of fey and human assistance to rout their enemy, rescue the library and the woodland, and restore peace to the forest?

Example 3
One Heiress Too Many

THE STORY ELEMENTS

- *Protagonist:* The fugitive daughter of ...
- *Situation:* ... a treasonous noble ...

- *Inciting Incident:* ... hides from the king's minions by posing as an alchemist in the home of her greatest enemy ...
- *Objective/ Stakes*: ... to escape detection long enough to expose the conspiracy that cost her father his life and her family their reputations.
- *Antagonist/ Opposition*: Her evil chamberlain stepfather is a rival guardian vying for her valuable wardship.
- *Central Conflict:* The fugitive heiress hides from the law in the belly of the beasts who are seeking her.

THE LOGLINE:

Can a fugitive heiress escape detection long enough to expose the conspiracy that cost her father his life and her family their fortune?

THE ELEVATOR PITCH:

The fugitive daughter of a treasonous noble hides from the king's minions by posing as an alchemist in the home of the high sheriff. Will she escape detection long enough to expose the conspiracy that cost her father his life and her family their fortune?

Example 4
Diary of a Honeymoon

THE STORY ELEMENTS

- *Protagonist:* A spoiled bride ...
- *Situation:* ... from a wealthy Edwardian family ...

- *Inciting Incident:* ... agrees to spend her honeymoon on her husband's grueling cross-country business trip.
- *Objective/ Stakes:* To share a romantic honeymoon with the man she loves.
- *Antagonist/ Opposition:* Expectations and realities of the journey collide with their fragile relationship.
- *Central Conflict:* A grueling road trip/honeymoon has the power to either strengthen their union or destroy the marriage before it begins.

THE LOGLINE:

Will their grueling road trip/honeymoon strengthen the newlyweds' union or will they split up before their marriage can even begin?

THE ELEVATOR PITCH:

In order to share a romantic honeymoon with her new husband, a spoiled bride from a wealthy family agrees to accompany him on his grueling cross-country business trip. As expectations and realities collide, will their journey strengthen their union, or will the newlyweds split apart before their marriage can even begin?

You've created all the elements of your story, now it's time to brainstorm your Logline and Elevator Pitches.

Your Elevator Pitch
~ Brainstorming Worksheet ~

YOUR PREMISE AS REFERENCE:

YOUR PROTAGONIST AS REFERENCE:

YOUR ANTAGONIST AS REFERENCE:

YOUR STORY ELEMENTS:

- *Protagonist:*
- *Situation:*
- *Inciting Incident:*
- *Objective/ Stakes:*
- *Antagonist/ Opposition:*
- *Central Conflict:*

YOUR LOGLINE:

YOUR ELEVATOR PITCH:

Congratulations!
You've finished the hard part! The rest is just doing what you love best! Giving your characters a goal, tossing them into the fray, and guiding them through the wilderness to the perfect ending you devised just for them.

The Wrap-Up

Whew! What a journey we've been on together!

Remember way back when your Idea was just a dim little Spark? Now that you've fanned it into a fiery Elevator Pitch, you have all the Story Elements you'll need to set the Special World of your novel ablaze. (Couldn't help running that metaphor into the ground!)

From the first Spark that ignited your Idea you've developed a solid foundation for your Story, and in the process learned:

- That brainstorming is an exercise in positive, creative freedom, where nothing is wrong and everything is right. Where every new idea becomes a deposit in your bank of possibilities.
- That the results of brainstorming the Origins of your Idea will reveal what your Idea Means to you—that it's the engine of your story.
- That you can use your list of brainstormed Theme Words to develop a dynamic Premise—the point you want your story to prove.
- That a well-orchestrated cast of Opposing Characters should include a Protagonist robust enough to withstand the powerful forces of the Antagonist, and a

Crucible rigorous enough to challenge them from Chapter One all the way to The End.

- That the Elevator Pitch you created from your Story Elements is your guide to a detailed synopsis, a map that lays out the dangerous route your Characters must take in order to reach their story goal.
- That you can use the tools in *First Spark* to brainstorm any book idea.
- That if you're stuck languishing midstream in your current novel, you can use any or all of the steps in *First Spark* to paddle your way out of the doldrums. Rediscover your Meaning, dissect the cause of your sagging middle, re-orchestrate your opposing characters, put your Elevator Pitch through its paces.
- That the end of our workshop is just the beginning of building your bestselling story!

I hope you've enjoyed brainstorming along with me and our intrepid Volunteer Brainstormers as much as I have. Most of all, I hope you can adapt the *First Spark* process to your own writing journey.

To help aid in the next part of your journey, I've included several additional resources.

- STEPS 1-6 for each Volunteer Brainstormer, assembled from the examples I used throughout the book.
- An expanded list of Theme Words from *Once Upon a Treasure Hunt.*
- A Guide to Brainstorming with Your Writing Group.
- A bibliography of my go-to writing craft books.
- Printable exercise worksheets.

Like any career worth pursuing, the journey we writers take from our idea to a published novel is equal parts joyful discovery, endless struggle, and intoxicating triumph. Fortunately, we don't ever have to travel alone.

I owe my own success to the writing community who so generously shows me the way every day, from craft, to networking, to the business itself. For that, I will be forever grateful.

Thank you so much for inviting me along to share the road with you. If you find a moment, please contact me at my website LindaNeedham.com where you'll also find my favorite tools and references, and can sign up for my writerly newsletter so we can keep in touch.

Happy brainstorming, and see you on the Bestseller List!

Linda

THE VOLUNTEER BRAINSTORMER EXAMPLES:

In the following four sections, you'll find STEPS 1-6 for each Volunteer Brainstormer, assembled from the examples I used throughout the book.

Example 1
The Vanishing Cyclist

STEP 1 – BRAINSTORMING THE ORIGIN AND THE IDEA

THE ORIGIN:

A writer who attended one of my workshops shared the spark of an idea that had followed her for years: From her position at a rest stop off the highway, the writer saw a bicyclist enter a short car tunnel carved into a California hillside. As cars occasionally entered and exited, she watched and waited for the cyclist to appear at the opposite end, but he never did.

THE IDEA:

A bicyclist enters a car tunnel and vanishes.

STEP 2 – BRAINSTORMING THE MEANING AND THE WHAT-IF

THE IDEA REMINDER:

A bicyclist enters a car tunnel and vanishes.

BRAINSTORMING THE MEANING:

Why did the incident of the vanishing cyclist intrigue the writer for such a long time?

During the workshop the writer's idea seemed to really resonate with the other attendees who collectively brainstormed a slew of questions:

- Was it an accident? Hit and run? A kidnapping? A domestic violence incident? A revenge killing? An alien abduction? A CIA extraction? Did he disappear through a time warp? Or a disguised door leading into a top-secret laboratory?
- Were they an innocent caught in the crossfire between warring factions? Did they fake their own disappearance? To outrun the law, debts, divorce? A tryst in the tunnel?
- If the cyclist died in the tunnel, what happened to the body? Where are the police, the emergency vehicles, the accident investigators? Who found the body? Was the cyclist ever reported missing? Why not?
- Who was the cyclist? An unfaithful spouse? An assassin from the future? Wealthy? Homeless? A doctoral student at a nearby university bio lab? Are they famous? Infamous? A billionaire venture capitalist? A well-respected spiritual leader? A muck-raking politician?

Whew! Brainstorming on overdrive! Great fun! Great story questions! Too many, of course, but determining the best of them is what the process is all about.

For the writer, the brainstorming exercise helped clarify for her that the fate of the vanishing cyclist was the element that had sparked her imagination all those decades after the incident.

THE MEANING:

The writer's concern for the fate of the cyclist elicits fear for their safety, doubt, uneasiness, curiosity, apprehension, suspense, giving the original Idea the source of its Meaning, and providing a very powerful central engine.

BRAINSTORMING THE WHAT-IF:

From the Meaning, the writer brainstormed the What-if:

- What if the fate of the cyclist exposes a dangerous conspiracy?
- What if the fate of the cyclist reveals an illicit love affair?
- What if the fate of the cyclist was a plot contrived by the cyclist to vanish in order to escape a worse fate? A crime? Criminals?
- What if the fate of the cyclist goes viral after a social media post ignites a global search that puts the original poster in danger?

THE WORKING WHAT-IF:

What if the fate of the cyclist exposes a dangerous conspiracy?

STEP 3 – BRAINSTORMING THEME WORDS

WHAT-IF REMINDER:

What if the fate of the cyclist exposes a dangerous conspiracy?

BRAINSTORMING THEME WORDS

- Dangerous, cover up, occult, suspected, unmarked, vanished, dark, camouflaged, truth, fragile, cloak-and-dagger, spy, genius, mysterious, enemy, illusion.

- Premonition, nameless, classified, shadowy, apprehensive, fate, expectation, undercover, conspiracy, overlooked, flight, sinister, pursue, fearless, betrayal.
- Threat, threaten, underground, fear, foreshadow, suspicion, clandestine, unknown, forewarn, ambush, covert, unseen, hope, portent, assault, trap, innocence, hunch.
- Prediction, foresee, dread, prophecy, waylay, mole, operative, traitor, malevolence, entrap, agent, patriot, inhospitable, set trap, courage, reckless, competition.
- Deception, hit and run, violence, missing, surprise, accident, kidnap, revenge, athletic, brutal, secret, hidden, lone, future, past, destiny, heroic, vulnerable.

STEP 4 – BRAINSTORMING THE PREMISE

WHAT-IF REMINDER:

What if the fate of the cyclist exposes a dangerous conspiracy?

BRAINSTORMING POSSIBLE PREMISES

- Uncompromising defiance in the face of impossible odds overcomes the fiercest enemy. (Positive trajectory)
- A fearless heart exposes the coldest conspiracy. (Positive trajectory)
- A reckless past leads to a sinister future. (Negative trajectory)
- A baffling mystery leads to death.
- A baffling mystery leads to forbidden love.
- An everyday activity cloaks a horrific truth.

THE WORKING PREMISE:

Uncompromising defiance in the face of impossible odds overcomes the fiercest enemy.

STEP 5 – THE CHARACTERS

THE WORKING PREMISE REMINDER:

Uncompromising defiance in the face of impossible odds overcomes the fiercest enemy.

BRAINSTORMING CHARACTERS FROM THE PREMISE:

Protagonist (A) *Uncompromising defiance in the face of impossible odds ...*

- Amateur sleuth, cyclist's sister, mother, ex-Marine cop, burned-out detective, group of misfit kids, the cyclist's cycling group, local FBI agent, cyclist's laboratory colleagues, cyclist's trainer, cyclist's spouse or lover, underappreciated newscaster.

Action (C) *... overcomes ...*

- (multiple story obstacles that reflect the premise) corruption, apathy, rivalry, red tape, inexperience, malfeasance, immorality, infamy, secret cipher, zealousness, coverup.

Antagonist (B) ... *the fiercest enemy*.

- Rogue military group, rival cycling group, local police department, foreign terrorists, global cabal of scientists, cartel, industrial espionage, Olympic team rival, cyclist's trainer, rogue government agency, vengeful lover, murderous spouse.

BRAINSTORMED CHARACTERS IN OPPOSITION:

Protagonist (A):

- The cyclist's sister is an ex-Marine, local FBI agent, and a member of her brother's cycling club.

Antagonist (B):

- A rogue governmental agency in league with a cabal of mad scientists.

STEP 6 – BRAINSTORMING THE ELEVATOR PITCH

THE STORY ELEMENTS:

- *Protagonist:* The missing cyclist's sister ...
- *Situation:* ... is an ex-marine, local FBI agent, and a member of her brother's competition cycling group.
- *Inciting Incident:* He goes missing after entering a remote car tunnel and hasn't been seen since. When the authorities refuse to investigate ...
- *Objective/ Stakes:* ... she vows to find her brother, no matter that it may cost her job or her life.

- *Antagonist/ Opposition:* Her investigation exposes a rogue government agency in league with a cabal of mad scientists who are threatening the world.
- *Central Conflict:* Will the missing cyclist's sister discover the fate of her brother in time to bring down the powerful enemy and save the world?

THE LOGLINE:

A young woman's search for her brother exposes a global conspiracy and awakens the wrath of a powerful enemy.

THE ELEVATOR PITCH:

When the authorities refuse to investigate her brother's disappearance during a cycling event, a young FBI agent risks everything to find him and expose those responsible. Will she discover the fate of her brother in time to bring down the powerful enemy and save the world?

Example 2
Library in the Woods

STEP 1 – BRAINSTORMING THE ORIGIN AND THE IDEA

THE ORIGIN:

Decades ago I became enchanted by a local TV news story about a retired librarian who opened a free 24/7 lending library in a charming, vintage Airstream trailer on her woodland property, which served her rural neighbors who couldn't get into town during regular library hours.

THE IDEA:

A 24-hour lending library in the woods.

STEP 2 – BRAINSTORMING THE MEANING AND THE WHAT-IF

THE IDEA REMINDER:

A 24-hour lending library in the woods.

BRAINSTORMING THE MEANING:

Why did the idea of the woodland library follow me so closely that I always included it as an example in my First Spark workshops?

- The librarian made me imagine an enchanting, twinkle-eyed elf who delighted in sharing her love of reading.
- Literacy is life, because our ability to communicate is everything that makes us human, and engages all of our senses: sight, touch, hearing, taste, smell, and that mystical sixth sense.
- The written word is our emotional connection to the past, the present, the future.
- Libraries are a repository of every human thought and experience.
- Folktales are often populated by mythical entities who live in a world of magic and enchantments. These entities take great pride in intersecting and interfering with human lives.

THE MEANING:

I loved the idea that whether library patrons arrived mid-day or in the middle of the night, they would find the windows aglow, the door unlocked, and a comfy chair, an open invitation for all to come read and browse and borrow. A truly magical setting.

The woods conjure mystical places, fey creatures, distorting sensations, misty creeks, shadows, stone, dappled sunlight, where mythical beings live and play, taunt and tease.

BRAINSTORMING THE WHAT-IF:

- What if the library is a safe house for the CIA?
- What if the library is a trysting place for a forbidden relationship?
- What if the librarian dies and her family wants to sell the property and close the library?

- What if the 24-hour lending library in the woods is a portal between the lands of fairy creatures and humans? (*An idea borrowed from an attendee at one of my bookstore workshops who emailed me afterward that she had used my woodland library idea for a paranormal short story.*)

THE WHAT-IF:

What if the 24-hour lending library in the woods is a portal between the land of fairy creatures and humans?

STEP 3 — BRAINSTORMING THE THEME WORDS

WHAT-IF REMINDER:

What if the 24-hour lending library in the woods is a portal between the lands of fairy creatures and humans?

BRAINSTORMING THEME WORDS:

- Enchantment, darkness, books, repository, shadowy, literacy, mystical, secrets, unexpected, welcoming, wonder, fairy tale, liberty, woodland, illiterate, library.
- Folklore, forest, oak, pine, fir, nighthawk, lending, otherworldly, deer, understory, owls, endow, squirrels, misty, borrow, beguile, belonging, magical, witchery.
- Spells, ensorcell, sorcery, bewitch, wizard, ancient, leafy glade, wildfire, smokey, campfire, charm, belief, escape, sprite, mysterious, portal, gateway, fable, spirit.
- Legend, myth, ghost, forbidden, mushrooms, forsake, ancient, arcane, fish out of water, between worlds, storyteller, stories, wicked, stepmother, maleficent, evil.

- Evildoing, goodness, kindness, virtue, generosity, grace, merciless, beauty, beast, monster, ogre, merciful, destiny, karma, purpose, make believe, love, malignant.

STEP 4 – BRAINSTORMING THE PREMISE

WHAT-IF REMINDER:

What if the 24-hour lending library in the woods is a portal between the lands of fairy creatures and humans?

BRAINSTORMING POSSIBLE PREMISES:

- An open heart invites goodness and light, a closed one only shadows.
- Evil enchants the strong as easily as the weak.
- The power of love is as ancient as wickedness.
- A welcoming library can open a closed mind and fill an empty heart.

THE WORKING PREMISE:

A free and welcoming library can open a closed mind and fill an empty heart.

STEP 5 – BRAINSTORMING THE CHARACTERS

THE WORKING PREMISE REMINDER:

A free and welcoming library can open a closed mind and fill an empty heart.

BRAINSTORMING CHARACTERS FROM THE PREMISE:

Protagonist (A) *A free and welcoming library ...*

- Fey librarian, firefighter, reluctant heir, forest ranger, retired teacher, librarian, fantasy author, logger, children, camper, book club member, ghost writer.

Action (C) *... can open ...*

- (Multiple story obstacles that reflect the premise) Belief, misbelief, nonbeliever, fear, prejudice, greed, illiteracy, intolerance, injustice, xenophobia, disdain, apartheid.

Antagonist (B) *... a closed mind and fill an empty heart.*

- Tourist board, logging company, inheritors, evil witch/wizard, warring fairy tribes, national park status, mundane fairy hunters, hunters, school board, county library system, church leaders, local courts.

BRAINSTORMED CHARACTERS IN OPPOSITION:

Protagonist (A):

- A forest ranger inherits a woodland library from her fey grandmother who started the book club fifty years before.

Antagonist (B):

- A local tourist board of mundane fairy hunters in league with the leader of an evil fairy tribe.

STEP 6 – BRAINSTORMING THE ELEVATOR PITCH

THE STORY ELEMENTS

- *Protagonist:* An idealistic young forest ranger who enjoys isolation ...
- *Situation:* ... inherits a woodland library from her fey librarian grandmother.
- *Inciting Incident:* Her siblings threaten her claim to the library, revealing plans to tear it down and clearcut the woodland.
- *Objective/ Stakes:* To save the library and the forest from destruction and expose the wicked plot ...
- *Antagonist/ Opposition:* ... set in motion by the local tourist board of mundane fairy hunters who are in league with the leader of an evil fairy tribe.
- *Central Conflict:* Can the young ranger muster a large enough cohort of fey and human assistance to rout their enemy, rescue the library and the woodland, and restore peace to the forest?

THE LOGLINE:

Can a young woman rescue her enchanted woodland library before it can be destroyed by an evil otherworldly rival?

THE ELEVATOR PITCH:

An idealistic young forest ranger inherits a woodland library from her fey librarian grandmother. With the backing of the leader of an evil fairy tribe, her siblings dispute her claim, threatening to destroy the library and clearcut the woodland. Will the ranger muster a large enough cohort of fey and human assistance to rout their enemy, rescue the library and the woodland, and restore peace to the forest?

Example 3
One Heiress Too Many

STEP 1 – BRAINSTORMING THE ORIGIN AND THE IDEA

THE ORIGIN:

As I learned while watching the *Showtime* series *The Tudors*, Henry VIII's fifth wife, the doomed Catherine Howard (beheaded), had grown up as a ward of her father's stepmother, the Dowager Duchess of Norfolk. Supervision was lax in the household, which included a dozen other children of various nobles, each sent to the Dowager to be educated and trained up in the ways of the nobility.

THE IDEA:

Warehousing the inconvenient sons and daughters of the nobility in a chaotic household far from home.

STEP 2 – BRAINSTORMING THE MEANING AND THE WHAT-IF

THE IDEA REMINDER:

Warehousing the inconvenient sons and daughters of the nobility in a chaotic household far from home.

BRAINSTORMING THE MEANING:

Why did the idea of warehousing inconvenient noble children stay with me over the years?

- I felt sorry for the hapless Catherine Howard, who was manipulated into a fatal marriage by her family who used her as a pawn in their thirst for political power.
- Family connections are the foundation of life, our closest relationships are the source of who we become.
- In order for children to correctly understand who they are and where they fit in the world, they need to feel cherished, be assured they belong.
- The cruelty of politics. An unsupervised childhood without boundaries. A carelessly cruel husband. An uncaring family.
- A child who grows up in an environment of emotional scarcity will constantly seek a place to belong.
- Searching to create a family of the people in her small sphere, she would make friends and enemies: kind and dangerous, life-long and transient, BFFs and scheming rivals, nurturing and deceitful.
- Also, I am a long-time, unapologetic Anglophile.

THE MEANING:

Family is everything, especially to a child who needs the support of people who care about her needs.

BRAINSTORMING THE WHAT-IF:

- What if she is the daughter of the king?
- What if this is an alternate universe, time-shifted?

- What if she has grown up wise and capable, despite the neglect of her family?
- What if she has learned a dangerous state secret?
- What if her powerful family loses its leader and she's evicted from the protection of the dower house?

THE WHAT-IF:

(Combines a few ideas from the above):

What if the leader of a young woman's powerful family is executed for treason, leaving her to flee for her life, with nothing but her wits and a dangerous state secret?

STEP 3 – BRAINSTORMING THE THEME WORDS

WHAT-IF REMINDER:

What if the leader of a young woman's powerful family is executed for treason, leaving her to flee for her life, with nothing but her wits and a dangerous state secret?

- Lonely, secrets, danger, scholarly, politics, fate, destiny, birthright, powerful, belonging, scarcity, deceit, treachery, conspiracy, mystery, abundance, neglect.
- Devious, undependable, shady, faithless, fickle, alchemy, loyalty, kinship, acceptance, potential, influence, privilege, sovereignty, domination, baseborn.
- Dominion, prerogative, inheritance, legacy, charade, occult, oracle, tainted, isolation, resilience, covert, clandestine, stealth, oppression, adversary, guardian.
- Oppression, privacy, marriage, expedient, avarice, fortune, legacy, title, nobility, greed, desire, love,

mistrust, scandal, legitimate, illegitimate, justice, benevolent.

- Grandiosity, masquerade, outlaw, family, heir, kindred, friends, honor, dignity, trust, deference, fealty, homage, obeisance, rank, reputation, pride, courage.

STEP 4 – BRAINSTORMING THE PREMISE

WHAT-IF REMINDER:

What if the leader of a young woman's powerful family is executed for treason, leaving her to flee for her life, with nothing but her wits and a dangerous state secret?

BRAINSTORMING POSSIBLE PREMISES:

- A noble heart can uplift the most villainous scoundrel.
- Steadfast courage vanquishes scandal and treachery.
- Destiny is a living thing, not anchored in history.
- A noble heart can turn destiny from scarcity to abundance.
- An open and forgiving heart can turn scarcity to abundance.
- Own your character, own your destiny.

THE WORKING PREMISE:

An open and forgiving heart can turn scarcity to abundance.

STEP 5 – BRAINSTORMING THE CHARACTERS

THE WORKING PREMISE REMINDER:

An open and forgiving heart can turn scarcity to abundance.

BRAINSTORMING CHARACTERS FROM THE PREMISE:

Protagonist (A) *An open and forgiving heart ...*

- A royal bastard, young widow, daughter of a noble family, abandoned orphan, rebellious bride, nun/postulant, tutor, disguised heiress, fugitive heiress, cut-purse, burglar, leader of a theft ring, alchemist, teacher.

Action (C) *... can turn ...*

- (multiple story obstacles that reflect the premise) mistrust, pride, grandiosity, stealth, avarice, consent, control, arrest writ, imprisonment, illness, scandal, proclamation, exposed.

Antagonist (B) *... scarcity to abundance.*

- The king, a rival, wicked relative, evil chamberlain, step-parent, chancery, a court rival, high sheriff, mother-in-law, half-sibling, rival guardians, evil bridegroom, false-hearted friend, bounty hunter.

BRAINSTORMED CHARACTERS IN OPPOSITION:

Protagonist (A):

- The fugitive daughter of a treasonous noble hides from the king's minions by posing as an alchemist in the home of the high sheriff.

Antagonist (B):

- An evil chamberlain and the heiress's cruel stepfather are vying for her valuable wardship.

STEP 6 – BRAINSTORMING THE ELEVATOR PITCH

THE STORY ELEMENTS

- *Protagonist:* The fugitive daughter of ...
- *Situation:* ... a treasonous noble ...
- *Inciting Incident:* ... hides from the king's minions by posing as alchemist in the home of her greatest enemy ...
- *Objective/ Stakes:* ... to escape detection long enough to expose the conspiracy that cost her father his life and her family their reputations.
- *Antagonist/ Opposition:* Her evil chamberlain stepfather is a rival guardian vying for her valuable wardship.
- *Central Conflict:* The fugitive heiress hides from the law in the belly of the beasts who are seeking her.

THE LOGLINE:

Can a fugitive heiress escape detection long enough to expose the conspiracy that cost her father his life and her family their fortune?

THE ELEVATOR PITCH:

The fugitive daughter of a treasonous noble hides from the king's minions by posing as an alchemist in the home of the high sheriff. Will she escape detection long enough to expose the conspiracy that cost her father his life and her family their fortune?

Example 4
Diary of a Honeymoon

STEP 1 – BRAINSTORMING THE ORIGIN AND THE IDEA

THE ORIGIN:

A number of years ago a close friend was given her great-aunt's letters, written in 1926 during her 2-month long, cross-county honeymoon/ husband's hospitality industry business trip.

The extended honeymoon was a working-trip, financed by the hospitality company the groom worked for at the time. His assignment was to leave holiday brochures in every motel along the ever-expanding network of paved roadways, made newly accessible to a growing number of ordinary folks by Henry Ford's affordable motor cars.

The bride mailed most of her letters to family members, asking them to save them for her. She also collected ephemera along the way, matchbooks, soap wrappers, postcards, local guides, maps, etc.

THE IDEA:

The travel diary adventures of a young couple embarking on their marriage.

STEP 2 – BRAINSTORMING THE MEANING AND THE WHAT-IF

THE IDEA REMINDER:

The travel diary adventures of a young couple embarking on their marriage in a new century.

BRAINSTORMING THE MEANING:

Why did the idea of a travel diary about a young couple embarking on their marriage in a new century so enchant me?

- The bride's letters are a delightful glimpse into the beginning of the romantic early years of touring the highways and byways of the US, the social mores of the times, and the early days of what I understand was a long and very happy marriage.
- Which also reminded me of the Lucy Ball and Desi Arnaz movie, *The Long, Long Trailer*, where the couple tows a huge travel trailer/honeymoon cottage across the country, hoping for a romantic journey but quickly discovering that love and marriage require compromise and forgiveness.
- Marriage is a journey of hills and valleys, spectacular vistas and comfy chairs, cliff-hangers and Elysian Fields.
- A honeymoon can be a magical time for a pair of newlyweds, a season of romance that holds reality at bay for a time.
- The exciting new century, the new technology, the honeymoon couple's new life together.

- The open road, expanding horizons.
- The early chapters of a marriage, forecasting the future, getting to know each other.

THE MEANING:

I love the idea of a newlywed bride documenting her honeymoon travels with her new husband, the ups and downs and sideways of the adventure of a lifetime.

Note: *This particular story idea can be told in a variety of ways:*

NON-FICTION:

- As a verbatim epistolary narration, chronological transcriptions of the letters, and/or images of the actual letters, accompanied by an editorial commentary on the couple's journey.
- A docu-diary, with a Point-of-View narrator, imagined dialog and conversations, citing portions of the letters and reactions to ephemera. This form allows for greater emotional engagement and connection with the reader than would a verbatim narration.

FICTION:

- As a novelist, I was instantly intrigued by the fictional possibilities inherent in the story of a young bride accompanying her groom on a months-long, cross-country business trip in the early days of automobile travel, where they are required to interact along the way with motel owners, small towns and big cities, roadside attractions, the new national park system, fellow travelers, road hazards, maintenance issues.

A COMBINATION OF FICTION AND NON-FICTION:

- Being a huge fan of vintage ephemera, I respond to both the monetary and emotional value of the collection.
- The basic idea of a cross-country honeymoon easily transports to any time period, past, present, future, into outer space, the jungle, set in the midst of unanticipated danger, the ocean, a wilderness, the Zombie Apocalypse, along the Oregon Trail ....

BRAINSTORMING THE WHAT-IF:

- What if the letters and memorabilia are published as a non-fiction record of an earlier time?
- What if possession of the collection is at the center of a dispute between family members?
- What if the letters contain private or embarrassing truths about the couple or the company he works for?
- What if the bride stumbles over a crime or mystery that hounds their entire journey?
- What if the spoiled bride has to be convinced to leave the comfort of home to accompany her new husband on his trip?
- What if the honeymoon couple sets out on the Oregon Trail?

THE WHAT-IF

What if the honeymoon mirrors their journey: starts out full of promise, encounters obstacles that make them question the wisdom of marrying each other, before love blossoms again through their shared hardships.

STEP 3 – BRAINSTORMING THE THEME WORDS

WHAT-IF REMINDER:

What if the honeymoon mirrors their journey: starts out full of promise, encounters obstacles that make them question the wisdom of marrying each other, before love blossoms again through their shared hardships?

BRAINSTORMING THEME WORDS:

- Honeymoon, memories, family, adventure, outreach, lovers, letters, cross-country, automobile, romance, journey, compromise, forgiveness, embarking, mapping.
- Diary, surprises, love, friendship, homesick, marriage, bride, groom, diary, legacy, travel, breakdown, hospitality, welcome, junket, progress, sightseeing, traverse.
- Share, experience, demanding, exhausting, stormy, regret, whining, tourist trap, explore, remote, frontier, pioneer, backwoods, broken-down, lonely, unexpected.
- Accident, accidental, amazing, unforeseen, excursion, rubberneck, vintage, insight, perception, adjustment, impression, empathy, ignorance, diversity, prejudice.
- Attitude, journal, observation, destination, happily ever after, relationship, promise, expansive, roadway, wedding, honeymoon, alliance, conjugal, majestic, assumption.

STEP 4 – BRAINSTORMING THE PREMISE

WHAT-IF REMINDER:

What if the honeymoon mirrors their journey: starts out full of promise,
encounters obstacles that make them question the wisdom of marrying
each other, before love blossoms again through their shared hardships?

BRAINSTORMING POSSIBLE PREMISES:

- A journey of 5,000 miles begins with the first step.
- Marriage is the most difficult journey of all.
- Life is a journey, not a destination.
- Marriage is a journey, not a destination.
- A marriage of a lifetime begins on the first day.

THE WORKING PREMISE:

Marriage is a journey, not a destination.

STEP 5 – BRAINSTORMING THE CHARACTERS

THE WORKING PREMISE REMINDER:

Marriage is a journey, not a destination.

BRAINSTORMING CHARACTERS FROM THE PREMISE:

Protagonist (A) *Marriage ...*

(Since the Protagonist is a Bride, our Volunteer brainstormed personality traits.)

- Reluctant, complaining, homebody, resistant, spoiled, adventurous, sheltered, bold, unafraid, reckless, modest, intrepid, showy, daddy's girl, rich.

Action (C) *... is a journey ...*

- No vacancy, road hazards, bad food, miscommunication, weather, hunger, flat tire, car camping, exhaustion, getting lost, theft, first argument.

Antagonist (B) *... not a destination.*

(The Antagonists are the bride's expectations and the cross-country trip itself.)

- Long hours on road, new husband, husband distracted, husband inattentive, road map, competing hotels, diner food quality, the clock/time, mean hotel manager, tour guide, small town police, husband's home office, the unknown.

BRAINSTORMED CHARACTERS – IN OPPOSITION:

Protagonist (A):

- A spoiled bride from a wealthy family accompanies her groom on a grueling cross-country trip in the 1920s.

Antagonist (B):

- (Expectations and the trip itself) Groom inattentive, distracted by road hazards, hotel managers, corrupt sheriff, fleas, and an unhappy bride.

STEP 6 – BRAINSTORMING THE ELEVATOR PITCH

THE STORY ELEMENTS

- *Protagonist:* A spoiled bride ...
- *Situation:* ... from a wealthy Edwardian family ...
- *Inciting Incident:* ... agrees to spend her honeymoon on her husband's grueling cross-country business trip.
- *Objective/ Stakes:* To share a romantic honeymoon with the man she loves.
- *Antagonist/ Opposition:* Expectations and realities of the journey collide with their fragile relationship.
- *Central Conflict:* A grueling road trip/honeymoon has the power to either strengthen their union or destroy the marriage before it begins.

THE LOGLINE:

Will their grueling road trip/honeymoon strengthen the newlyweds' union, or will they split up before their marriage can even begin?

THE ELEVATOR PITCH:

In order to share a romantic honeymoon with her new husband, a spoiled bride from a wealthy family agrees to accompany him on his grueling cross-country business trip. As expectations and realities collide, will their journey strengthen their union, or will the newlyweds split apart before their marriage can even begin?

Once Upon a Treasure Hunt
Images - Textures - Tone - POV

Jack

Dragon: Dragon, draco, worm, serpent, beast, brute, chimera, demon, heathen, monster, ogre, rascal, savage, scoundrel, villain,

Underground: Under, nether, nethermost, lowermost, beneath, underneath, below, down, hell, clandestine, cover, furtive, secret,

Deep: Depth, profound, depression, pit, shaft, hollow, well, crater, abyss, bowels of the earth, bottomless, hell, soundings, draft, submerse, plummet, probe, plunge, submerge, deep-bosomed, sink, bury, subterranean, knee-deep, soundless, fathomless, unfathomed, unfathomable, abysmal, well-deep, down-reaching, yawning, whelming, sonorous, hole,

Base: Basement, bedrock, foundation, substructure, ground, earth, bilge, sump, culet, nadir, low,

Cave: Concave, dip, hollow, indentation, intaglio, cavity, dent, dint, dimple, antrum, sap, colliery, caisson, trough, cup, basin, cave, cavern, cove, grot, grotto, alcove, burrow, tunnel, passage,

Mining: Miner, scoop, gouge, dig, delve, excavate, undermine, stave in, horse path, burrow, channel, prod, discover, dredge, drill, drive, exhume, expose, extract, gibe, hollow, hollow out, jab, mine, penetrate, pierce, poke, punch, quarry, reveal, root, shovel, spade, stab, thrust, uncover, well,

Mining elements: Sulphur, coal, lead, silver, gold, tin, iron, ore, iron-stone, slag, carbon,

Color/Texture: Rust, sulphur, silver, cold, hard, rough, grainy, pitted, gravely, coarse, gritty, studded, eroded, raspy, fretted, rifled, grazed, scuffed, polished, burnished,

Movement: Worm, wiggle, twist, squirm, slither, undulate, hook, jog, kink, ply, turn, billow, anchor, clasp, clip, crook, grapple, angle, bow, buckle, bend, clamp, capture, catch, crampon, curve, curl, enmesh, entangle, ensnare, lash, moor, latch, lock, lodge, mooring, secure, snare, spiral, latch, encircle, circle, circling, climb, coil, braid, entwine, intertwine, plait, weave, curve, enlarge, gyre, helical, helix, increase, mount, multiply, noose, loop, scrolled, swirl, twine, twirl, whirl, wind, winding, roll, careen, knit, mesh, lurch, nap, reel, snake, stagger, sway, thread, totter, warp,

Mairey

Spirit: Sprite, elfin, invisible, furtive, apparition, archangel, phantom, fairy, dwarf, brownie, fay, gnome, leprechaun, mermaid, nereid, nymph, pixie, siren, sylph, temptress,

Elements: Air, wind, vent, ventilate, voice, melody, song, tune, storm, breeze, ambience, aura, breath, broadcast, charisma, charm, circulate, fly, soar, free, airy, light-hearted, fire, blaze, beacon, burn, candle, cook, detonate, conflagration, enthusiasm, flame, hearth, light, ardor, arouse, excite, fervor, fireside, firestorm, force, fuel, ignite, induce, inferno, inflame, inspire, intensity, kiln, kindle, pitch, power, rouse, spark, stoke, trigger, wildfire, zeal, water, creek, stream cascade, current, brook, branch, flexible, graceful, liquid, solution, earth, fluid, supple, easy, effortless, elegant

Duty: Accountability, assignment, burden, commitment, concern, imperative, mission, obligation, responsibility, task, toll, tribute, tradition, business, charge, chore, custody, custom, job, liability, office, payment, trust, belief, errand, yoke, debt, engagement, bondage, brace, legacy, inheritance, bequest, birthright, endowment, estate, heritage, history, reputation, will, indenture, prison, serfdom,

Thievery: Sneak, steal, trick, evade, artifice, caper, con, bandit, hoodlum, robbery, piracy, larceny, lurk, prowl, skulk, slink, smuggle, bootleg, abduct, cheat, defraud, embezzle, filch, forge, heist, misappropriate, pilfer, pirate, poach, pinch, purloin, rustle, pocket, snitch, swindle, swipe, take,

Secret: Arcane, baffling, clandestine, classified, concealed, confidence, confidential, conundrum, covert, cryptic, enigma, esoteric, hidden, hide, inner, innermost, inside, intimate, isolated, mysterious, obscure, personal, private, privy, puzzle, puzzling, riddle, secluded, sly, sneaky, stealthy, surreptitious, ulterior, undercover, undisclosed, unexpressed, unrevealed, untold, veiled,

Woodland: Green, forest, woods, growth, park, garden, preserve, common, grass, meadow, thicket, weald, heath, herbage, pasture, field, moor, down, fen, grove, underbrush, scrub, bush,

Search: Hunt, pursue, probe, investigate, seek, inquiry, tail, question, examine, grill, sift through, pry, delve, burrow, root, inspect, survey, review, scan, skim, dip into, touch upon, consider, appraise, quest, explore, dig, forage, grope, frisk trace, stalk, trail, follow, track, nose,

BRAINSTORMING
WITH YOUR WRITING GROUP

*As we've seen with our Volunteer Brainstormers, multiple brainstormers
are sometimes more effective than just one!*

THE GROUP ORIGIN

My beloved group of best friends started hanging out together
more than twenty years ago at the Romance Writers of America
annual conferences. Each time our then-mutual publisher organized an off-site booksigning, hosted schmooze parties with
industry bigwigs, or threw lavish dinners for us at incredible
venues, the six of us would naturally gravitate to each other. In the
wake of COVID-19, we discovered Zoom and now meet live every
other week, though we live almost 11,000 miles apart.

Now that we no longer attend conferences, our annual week-
long writing retreat at the beach has become the highlight of the
year. We quietly work on our own projects during the day, then
after a fabulously noisy home-cooked dinner, we spend two hours
brainstorming one writer's next project, with each of us getting a
session during the week. At times, we've come away with 11 or 12
new plot lines in a single week!

Even with a combined 170+ years in the business and more
than 260 published novels among us–most of them *New York Times*

and *USA Today* bestsellers–these brainstorming sessions have nurtured dozens of traditionally and independently published books that might not have become bestsellers, let alone exist, without my fabulous group of writer friends.

We don't use the *First Spark* process during our beach retreat sessions, but the effect is the same. We take an idea, and/or a set of characters, and/or a situation and toss around what-ifs and story elements until the writer has a workable storyline, or two, or sometimes three!

My point is that brainstorming, alone or with others, is a fabulous way to strengthen your storytelling muscles!

THE GROUP IDEA

Because *First Spark* originated as an in-person, interactive workshop with a room full of conference attendees, it's easy to adapt for brainstorming sessions with your own writer's group.

TIPS AND SUGGESTIONS FOR YOUR OWN BRAINSTORMING SESSION:

- Start every session with a fun and freeing, communal, out-loud warm-up exercise of your own devising.
- Appoint a moderator to keep everyone on task through the process.
- To ward off total chaos, no more than 6 to 8 participants.
- Create a comfortable place to spread out, such as a dining room table, or at a beach house/mountain cabin retreat.
- A whiteboard or an easel with a large pad of paper lends itself to big concepts and the space to scrawl lots of ideas.

- Audio record the session to preserve the ideas that might escape in the fracas. Individuals can record their own sessions.
- Print a set of brainstorming worksheets from this book for each brainstormer, or create a set of your own that best fits your writing needs.
- *NOTE*: The group may choose to complete the entire brainstorming process, from Idea through Elevator Pitch, with a single writer before going on to the next.

HELPFUL GUIDELINES:

- Anything goes. *Anything*.
- The more unconventional, the greater the variety, the better.
- An open space invites creativity.
- Quantity not quality, quality comes later.
- Not the time to be judgmental.
- Launch one idea off another.
- Where appropriate, combine ideas to create new ones.

STEP 1 – THE IDEA

- Complete the exercise individually, jot, jot, jot.
- Invite everyone to share their Idea with the group.
- Refrain from discussion at this point.

STEP 2 – THE MEANING

- Complete the exercise individually.
- Invite everyone to share their Meaning and What-if with the group.
- Refrain from discussion at this point.

STEP 3 – THEME WORDS

- Agree on which writer's Step 1-2 exercise the group wants to brainstorm together.
- Appoint a scribe who will quickly scrawl the hurricane of Theme Words that is about to be unleashed. Works fine for the chosen writer to be the scribe.
- Brainstorm the Theme Words as group.
- Fling words about. Be wild. Look at every possible side of the theme.

NEXT: Decide how best to proceed from this point in the process:

1) Continue brainstorming the next step or steps with that same person, stopping at an agreed upon step; or
    2) Repeat Step 3 with a new person, until everyone has a list of brainstormed Theme Words. Share the results as you go.

STEP 4 – PREMISE

- Agree on whose Step 3 Theme Words exercise the group wants use to brainstorm their Premise.
- Make the list of Theme Words visible to everyone during Step 4.

- Appoint a scribe to record all of the many derivations of the Premise to come. (This time don't use the person whose Premise you're brainstorming; it's too distracting for them.)
- Brainstorm as group.
- The list will be long and might end up looking something like a crazy Wordle game chart:

Good overcomes evil.
Good works conquer evil doings.
A good heart is invincible,
an evil soul corrupts from within.

NEXT: Decide again how best to proceed from this point in the process:

1) Continue brainstorming the next step or steps with that same person, stopping at an agreed upon step; or

2) Repeat Step 4 with a new person, until everyone has brainstormed their final Premise. Share the results as you go.

STEP 5 – CHARACTERS

- Agree on whose Step 4 Premise exercise the group wants use to brainstorm their Characters.
- Make the final Premise visible to everyone.
- Appoint a scribe to record the entire list of Characters A and B. (Again, don't use the person whose Premise you're brainstorming; it's too distracting for them.)
- Brainstorm both Character types as group.

NEXT: Decide again how best to proceed from this point in the process:

1) Continue brainstorming the next step or steps with that same person, stopping at an agreed upon step; or

2) Repeat Step 5 with a new person, until everyone has brainstormed their Characters. Share the results as you go.

STEP 6 – ELEVATOR PITCH

- Agree on whose Step 5 Character exercise the group wants use to brainstorm the Elevator Pitch.
- Make the Character list visible to everyone.
- Let the person whose Elevator Pitch you're using be their own scribe and lead the brainstorming.
- Brainstorm the Elevator Pitch as a group.
- Repeat Step 6 with a new person, until everyone has brainstormed their Elevator Pitch. Share the results as you go.

NOTE:

These are just suggestions, of course! Please adapt the process to your own group's needs. I would love to hear how you do it! And how many titles you produce!

RESOURCES
AND YOUR WRITING COMMUNITY

MY #1 ADVICE:

> Join a writing community, online or in-person! You'll never regret it!

MY BOOKS — THE EXAMPLES

Once Upon a Treasure Hunt

I used examples from *Treasure Hunt* throughout *First Spark.*

The Maiden Bride, a Castle Keep Romance

I used TMB in Step 3 Theme Words to illustrate using symbols to describe the essence of the conflict between the two main characters.

A FEW OF MY GO-TO WRITING BOOKS:

Creating Blockbusters!: How to Generate and Market Hit Entertainment for TV, Movie, Video Games, and Books, by Gene Del Vecchio

An expansive "battlefield manual" for authors/screenwriters with a story idea that needs to be told. A gem.

The Art of Dramatic Writing, by Lajos Egri

My favorite deep dive into developing fully-realized characters and the conflict that arises from the pursuit of their goals.

The Writer's Journey, 3rd Edition, by Christopher Vogler

The life-changing, ah-ha! writing book that set me on the road to the bestseller list. The Hero's Journey told with loads of examples that help clarify every step.

The Spark of Your Idea Exercise
~ Brainstorming Worksheet~

Briefly—very briefly—describe a setting, situation, character, event, or anything at all that has intrigued you enough to consider creating a story around it.

Just jot! Don't compose—jot, jot, jot! This isn't a writing exercise. The basic Idea only.

THE ORIGIN:

YOUR IDEA:

The Meaning & What-if
~ Brainstorming Worksheet ~

List as many elements as you can think of that give Meaning to your Idea.

Once you've got 10-20 meaningful elements, choose the one that touches you most deeply, then create a compelling What-if story question.

(Add, subtract, or change, as your understanding of the Meaning and What-if of your Idea evolves—which it will.)

BRAINSTORM YOUR MEANING:

BRAINSTORM YOUR WHAT-IF:

Your Theme Words
~ Brainstorming Worksheet ~

With your Meaning and What-if in mind from Step 2, list single words, simple terms, or phrases you associate with your original Idea in Step 1.

Take your time. No rush. Brainstorm alone or with your writers group, or your family. Leave the exercise for a few days, then add more words as you think of them. List words, terms and phrases, positives & negatives. Dig into a thesaurus, one of my favorite places to discover Theme Words.

Don't analyze. No judgment. No right or wrong. No holds barred.

BRAINSTORM YOUR THEME WORDS

Your Premise
~ Brainstorming Worksheet ~

PREMISE TEMPLATE:

- One of your characters will be driven to act out the A Part of your Premise.
- The opposing character or force will act out the B Part of the Premise.
- The Action (Part C) of your story represents the essence of the conflict.

BRAINSTORM YOUR PREMISE:

YOUR WORKING PREMISE:

Your Characters
~ Brainstorming Worksheet ~

- Refer to your Theme Words as you brainstorm a list of Protagonists who might represent the (A) side of your premise.
- Brainstorm the same for possible Antagonists (B).
- Use the Action (C) column to brainstorm a list of thematic obstacles that will confound and impede your characters during the course of their journey.

PROTAGONIST–THE A PART OF YOUR PREMISE:

THE ACTION–THE C PART OF YOUR PREMISE:

ANTAGONIST– THE B PART OF YOUR PREMISE:

Your Elevator Pitch
~ Brainstorming Worksheet ~

YOUR PREMISE AS REFERENCE:

YOUR PROTAGONIST AS REFERENCE:

YOUR ANTAGONIST AS REFERENCE:

YOUR STORY ELEMENTS:

- *Protagonist:*
- *Situation:*
- *Inciting Incident:*
- *Objective/ Stakes:*
- *Antagonist/ Opposition:*
- *Central Conflict:*

YOUR LOGLINE:

YOUR ELEVATOR PITCH:

Congratulations!

You've finished the hard part! The rest is just doing what you love best! Giving your characters a goal, tossing them into the fray, and guiding them through the wilderness to the perfect ending you devised just for them.

Also By LINDA NEEDHAM

LindaNeedham.com/books

THE LEGEND OF NIMWAY HALL: THE SERIES

1940 — Josie

1940 — Josie & Gideon's Christmas Wedding

THE GENTLEMAN ROGUES: THE SERIES

The Pleasure of Her Kiss

A Scandal to Remember

Marry the Man Today

THE MEDIEVALS:

For My Lady's Kiss

Her Secret Guardian

The Maiden Bride

The Bride Bed

THE REGENCY & VICTORIANS:

My Wicked Earl

Ever His Bride

Once Upon a Treasure Hunt (Original title: *The Wedding Night*)

ANTHOLOGIES

Baby Shoes:

100 Stories by 100 Authors (Flash in a Flash)

WRITING REFERENCES

Brainstorming Your Novel: From First Spark to Blockbuster

ABOUT LINDA

LindaNeedham.com/about

I began my journey on the road to romance writing in 1972 with an overcooked Thanksgiving turkey and my nose buried in a delicious copy of Kathleen Woodiwiss's first novel, *The Flame and the Flower*. Reading had always been one of my favorite obsessions, but Woodiwiss had for the first time fused the sweeping majesty of history with the sensual power of romance, and from that moment the romance novel industry went into high gear and was changed forever. I was desperately hooked on historical romance and soon after began secretly writing my own romance novel. I had a lot to learn!

Nearly 25 years after that fateful Thanksgiving weekend of 1972, my unpublished manuscript, *For My Lady's Kiss* won 1st place in six romance writing competitions, 2nd and 3rd place in six other competitions, and the 1995 Romance Writers of America's Golden Heart for Long Historical. Two months later the book sold, along with a one-line proposal for my second book, *Ever His Bride*, both to Avon Books, and, in February 1997, to my great delight, my first novel—*For My Lady's Kiss* was released! Many more books have followed, with five hitting the USA Today Bestseller list.

Of course, like every author, I started writing in early grade school, as soon as I realized that I could put my own words together to make my own stories, just like the authors of my favorite childhood books—*Beautiful Joe* and *Heidi* and the *Nancy Drew* mysteries.

My love for storytelling eventually led me to a bachelor's degree in Theatre Arts where I gained a deep understanding of character development, dialogue, scene-shaping and plotting techniques. I'm also a playwright, one of the lucky few who have had full productions of their works—seven full length musicals, four revues and two full-length plays.

I write full-time from my home office near Portland, Oregon. And when I'm not writing, I've been known to direct plays and musicals, garden 'til I drop, spoil my two grandkids, take extended research treks with my hero husband and participate in K9 Nose Work with Winnie, our Portuguese Water Dog.

facebook.com/LindaNeedhamAuthor
instagram.com/authorlindaneedham
pinterest.com/TheLindaNeedham
goodreads.com/Linda_Needham
tiktok.com/@lindaneedham_authorrom